RUSSIAN SHORT STORIES FOR BEGINNERS

20 Captivating Short Stories to Learn Russian & Grow Your Vocabulary the Fun Way!

Easy Russian Stories

Lingo Mastery

www.LingoMastery.com

CONTENTS

Introduction 1

CHAPTER I – Как мы встретились — How We Met 7

Краткое содержание истории...........................10

Summary of the story...10

Vocabulary 11

Questions about the story 15

Answers 17

CHAPTER II – Идеальный писатель — A Perfect Writer...........18

Краткое содержание истории...........................21

Summary of the story...21

Vocabulary 22

Questions about the story 25

Answers 27

CHAPTER III – Спасатели — Rescuers 28

Краткое содержание истории...........................31

Summary of the story...31

Vocabulary...32

Questions about the story 35

Answers 37

CHAPTER IV – Подарок — A Present **38**

Краткое содержание истории 41

Summary of the story.. 41

Vocabulary 42

Questions about the story 45

Answers 47

CHAPTER V – Менделеев — Mendeleev...............................**48**

Краткое содержание истории 50

Summary of the story.. 50

Vocabulary 52

Questions about the story 55

Answers 57

CHAPTER VI – Ты счастлива? — Are You Happy?......................**58**

Краткое содержание истории 61

Summary of the story.. 61

Vocabulary 62

Questions about the story 65

Answers 67

CHAPTER VII – Всё к лучшему — It's All for the Best...............**68**

Краткое содержание истории 71

Summary of the story.. 71

Vocabulary.. 72

Questions about the story 75

Answers 77

CHAPTER VIII – Настоящий мужчина — A Real Man 78

Краткое содержание истории...81

Summary of the story...81

Vocabulary 82

Questions about the story 85

Answers 87

CHAPTER IX – Богатый человек — A Rich Man 88

Краткое содержание истории...91

Summary of the story...91

Vocabulary 93

Questions about the story 96

Answers 98

CHAPTER X – Достоевский — Dostoevsky.............................99

Краткое содержание истории...101

Summary of the story...101

Vocabulary 102

Questions about the story 105

Answers 107

CHAPTER XI – Внешность бывает обманчива — Appearances Can Be Deceptive **108**

Краткое содержание истории 111

Summary of the story........................... 111

Vocabulary 112

Questions about the story 115

Answers 117

CHAPTER XII – Настоящий детектив — True Detective...........**118**

Краткое содержание истории 120

Summary of the story........................... 120

Vocabulary 121

Questions about the story 124

Answers 126

CHAPTER XIII – Важный диалог — A Real Dialogue **127**

Краткое содержание истории 129

Summary of the story........................... 129

Vocabulary 130

Questions about the story 133

Answers 135

CHAPTER XIV – Мамина свобода — Mom's Freedom **136**

Краткое содержание истории 139

Summary of the story........................... 139

Vocabulary 140

Questions about the story 143

Answers 145

CHAPTER XV – Новогоднее чудо — New Year's Miracle **146**

Краткое содержание истории................................. 148

Summary of the story.. 148

Vocabulary 149

Questions about the story 152

Answers 154

CHAPTER XVI – Чехов — Chekhov **155**

Краткое содержание истории................................. 157

Summary of the story.. 157

Vocabulary 158

Questions about the story 161

Answers 163

CHAPTER XVII – Мечта — A Dream **164**

Краткое содержание истории................................. 167

Summary of the story.. 167

Vocabulary 168

Questions about the story 172

Answers 174

CHAPTER XVIII – Свободное место — An Empty Seat............**175**

Краткое содержание истории 177

Summary of the story.. 177

Vocabulary.. 178

Questions about the story 181

Answers.. 183

CHAPTER XIX – Выбор — A Choice.................................**184**

Краткое содержание истории 187

Summary of the story.. 187

Vocabulary.. 188

Questions about the story 191

Answers.. 193

CHAPTER XX – Мой урок. Твой урок — My Lesson. Your Lesson **194**

Краткое содержание истории 197

Summary of the story.. 197

Vocabulary.. 199

Questions about the story 202

Answers.. 204

MORE FROM LINGO MASTERY **205**

Conclusion...**207**

INTRODUCTION

So you want to learn Russian? That's awesome!

Like any other foreign language, it's going to open the doors to discovering a completely new culture. Whether you're learning Russian for work, studies or fun, the knowledge of the language will broaden your mind, let you meet new people, and will become a new page in the thrilling book of your self-development.

Heard about Russian being impossibly hard to learn? That might be true. But that's what we're here for. Rely on this book that was written with your needs in mind and accept the challenge without any fear or doubts.

What is the following book about?

We've written this book to cover an important issue that seems to affect every new learner of the Russian tongue — a lack of helpful reading material. While in English you may encounter tons (or gigabytes, in our modern terms) of easy and accessible learning material, in Russian you will usually and promptly be given tough literature to read by your teachers, and you will soon find yourself consulting your dictionary more than you'd want to. Eventually, you'll find yourself bored and uninterested in continuing, and your initially positive outlook may soon turn sour.

Our goal with this book will be to supply you with useful, entertaining, helpful and challenging material that will not only allow you to learn the language but also help you pass the time and make the experience less formal and more fun — like any particular lesson should be. We will not bore you with grammatical notes, spelling or structure: the book has been well-written and revised to ensure that it covers those aspects without having to explain them in unnecessarily complicated rules like textbooks do.

If you've ever learned a new language through conversational methods, teachers will typically just ask you to practice speaking. Here, we'll teach you writing and reading Russian with stories. You'll learn both how to read it *and* write it with the additional tools we'll give you at the end of each story.

The stories are for Beginners. What does it mean?

We don't want the word to be misleading for you. When thinking about you as a beginner, we focused on combining two things:

1. provide you with easy to understand words and structures;
2. avoid simplistic content.

Judging by our extensive experience, it's impossible to make any impressive progress by dealing with the material that you are absolutely comfortable with. Dive into the unknown, make an effort, and you'll be rewarded.

To make things easier for you, we picked only common words – no rocket science, that's for sure. You won't encounter any complex sentences with multiple clauses and prepositions.

Just take the last step — apply your diligence and work hard to go over to the next level.

The suggested steps of working with the book

1. First, just read the story. Chances are you already know many words.

2. Then read it again, referring to the vocabulary. Note that our vocabulary is much easier to use than a conventional dictionary because:

   a) the words are listed in order of their appearance in the text;
   b) the translations are given in the very form you find them in the text;
   c) the most complex words are given as word combinations to let you grasp the grammatical structure.

3. Now that you think you understand the major plot of the story, check yourself by referring to the summary of the story that is provided both in Russian and English.
4. Go over to the Questions section to check if you've understood the details.
5. Check if you were right in the Answers section.
6. And at last — time to enjoy. Read the story once again, getting pleasure from the feeling of great achievement. You deserved it!

What if I don't understand everything?

Remember — understanding each and every word is not your goal. Your goal is to grasp the essence of the story and enrich your vocabulary. It is **absolutely normal** that you may not understand some words or structures and that sometimes you may ultimately not entirely understand what the story is about. We're here to *help* you in any way we can.

If you don't know some word and it's not in bold (i.e., not in the vocabulary list), then

- You may have already encountered it but in a different form. Challenge your attention!
- The word may be of an international character. What could the word 'такси' – [taksi] mean? Right! It's 'taxi'.
- Use the context. Let's turn to the 'taxi' example again. What can you possibly do with a taxi? Right, you can call or catch it!

Other recommendations for readers
of *Russian Short Stories for Beginners*

Before we allow you to begin reading, we have a quick list of some other recommendations, tips and tricks for getting the best out of this book.

1. Read the stories without any pressure: feel free to return to parts you didn't understand and take breaks when necessary. This is like any fantasy, romance or sci-fi book you'd pick up, except with different goals.
2. Feel free to use any external material to make your experience more complete: while we've provided you with plenty of data to help you learn, you may feel obliged to look at textbooks or search for more helpful texts on the internet — do not think twice about doing so! We even recommend it.
3. Find other people to learn with: while learning can be fun on your own, it definitely helps to have friends or family joining you on the tough journey of learning a new language. Find a like-minded person to accompany you in this experience, and you may soon find yourself competing to see who can learn the most!

4. Try writing your own stories once you're done: all of the material in this book is made for you to learn not only how to read, but how to write as well. Liked what you read? Try writing your own story now, and see what people think about it!

FREE BOOK!

Free Book Reveals The 6 Step Blueprint That Took Students

From Language Learners To Fluent In 3 Months

One last thing before we start. If you haven't already, head over to LingoMastery.com/hacks and grab a copy of our free Lingo Hacks book that will teach you the important secrets that you need to know to become fluent in a language as fast as possible.

Now, without further ado, enjoy these 20 Russian Stories for Beginners.

Good luck, reader!

CHAPTER I

Как мы встретились — How We Met

Я и моя **жена вместе** уже **тридцать** лет. У нас были **разные времена. Иногда** мы **ссорились.** Иногда у нас было **мало денег.** Иногда мы **делали ошибки.** Но у нас была **самая главная вещь — любовь.**

Она помогала **решать** любые **проблемы. Например, около двух лет** я был **безработным.** Что **бы** сказала обычная **женщина**?

— Серж, иди и **найди работу**! Мне нужно **кормить** детей!

Но моя Лена не обычная женщина. Она не **жаловалась.** Она знала, что это **не навсегда.** И она была **права**! Я **написал книгу.** Книга **стала** очень **популярной.** Так я стал **писателем.** Иногда у меня не было **вдохновения.** И **опять** — мало денег. Но Лена **поддерживала** меня.

Или вот **ещё один пример.** Лене было **тридцать пять.** Она часто **плохо себя чувствовала.** Врачи сказали, что у неё **рак.** Мы **боролись пять** лет. И мы **победили**!

Короче говоря, у нас была насыщенная **жизнь. Благодаря** любви. Но моя **история** не об этом. Моя история о том, как мы встретились. Мы **обожаем рассказывать** эту историю! **Многие** не **верят** нам.

Итак, мне было **девятнадцать.** Я **поступил** в университет в **Париже.** Я жил **в общежитии** для студентов. Я **мечтал** стать

богатым и знаменитым. Я мечтал и о любви **тоже**. Но **тогда** я не знал, **что это**.

Я встретил Лену в университете. Я **сразу заметил** её. Она **отличалась от** других **девушек**. **Оказалось**, она **студентка по обмену из России**. Она в Париже **на год**. Мне было **легко общаться** с ней. Я **показал** ей **город**. **Познакомил** со своими друзьями. Мы очень хорошо **понимали друг друга**.

Романтические чувства? **Странно**, но **в начале** у меня их не было. **Но через полгода** я понял, что Лена — не мой друг. **Может**, я люблю её? Ещё через месяц мы **начали встречаться**. Всё было **здорово**. **Долгие** прогулки, **поцелуи**, **стихи**, но... Я знал, что Лена **уедет**. Она **не могла остаться** в Париже.

Нет, могла!

— **Если** ты **женишься** на ней, — сказал мой друг, — она **сможет** остаться.

Жениться? Но мне **только** девятнадцать! Да, Лена **удивительная** девушка. Но есть и **другие. А что если** она не моя **судьба**?

— Ты любишь её? — спросил мой друг.
— Да, думаю, да, — ответил я.
— Тогда **в чём проблема**?

Теперь я знаю: я **боялся ответственности**. Я боялся **потерять свободу**. Я **не сделал предложение**. Мы **обменялись адресами**.

— **Пиши** мне. **Обещай**! — сказала она.

Я обещал и я писал ей... **Несколько** месяцев. А потом... **Учёба**, друзья... Нет, я **не забыл** о ней. Я **заставил себя** забыть.

«Ты **не поедешь** в Россию. Она не поедет **во Францию**. Ты ещё очень **молодой**. Есть девушки **лучше Лены**», — говорил я себе.

Это была **огромная** ошибка! **Прошло три года.** Я встречался с несколькими девушками. Я всегда **сравнивал** их с Леной. Она **лучшая!** Я **так поздно** понял это! Или не поздно?

— Я напишу ей! — сказал я своему другу. — Я **извинюсь.** Я буду **умолять!** Она **простит** меня. Я **брошу** всё!

— Ты **попросишь** её **переехать** в Париж?

— **Это не важно.** Я могу жить в России. С Леной — даже **в Антарктиде.**

Я написал **длинное письмо!** Лена **хранит** его. Но Лена **прочитала** его только **через пять лет.** Она **сменила** адрес и письмо **вернулось** ко мне.

Как я мог **найти** её? Я даже не знал её **фамилию. Сколько** Лен живёт в России? А может, она уже **в другой стране**?

Прошло пять лет. У моих друзей были **семьи.** Я был **уверен,** что Лена **вышла замуж.** Я был **одинок.** Мой друг однажды сказал мне:

— Сходи на **свидание вслепую.**

«Почему нет», — подумал я.

Свидание было в кафе. Я **немного опоздал.** Девушка **уже пришла.** Я видел только её **голову** и **спину**, но я **сразу узнал** её. Это была Лена! Моя Лена!

Как я заставил её простить меня? Это уже **другая история**...

Краткое содержание истории

Серж и его жена Лена вместе уже много лет. Эта история о том, как они встретились. Сержу было девятнадцать. Он учился в Париже. Лена была студенткой по обмену из России. Вскоре Серж и Лена начали встречаться. Но Лена должна была уехать из Франции.

Они обменялись адресами. Серж обещал писать ей. Через несколько месяцев он заставил себя забыть Лену. Он не был готов уехать в Россию. Он знал, что Лена не сможет приехать во Францию.

Через три года он понял, что Лена лучшая девушка. Он написал ей. Письмо пришло обратно. Лена сменила адрес. Через пять лет он встретил её на свидании вслепую. Серж заставил Лену простить его, но это уже другая история.

Summary of the story

Serge and his wife Lena have been together for many years already. This story is about how they met each other. Serge was nineteen. He was studying in Paris. Lena was an exchange student from Russia. Soon Serge and Lena began to date. But Lena had to leave France.

They exchanged their addresses. Serge promised to write to her. In a few months, he made himself forget about Lena. He wasn't ready to go to Russia. He knew she wouldn't be able to go to France.

In three years, he understood that Lena is the best girl. He wrote to her. The letter came back. She'd changed the address. In five years, he met her on a blind date. He made her forgive him, but it's a different story.

Vocabulary

- **как мы встретились**: how we met
- **жена**: wife
- **вместе**: together
- **тридцать**: thirty
- **разные времена**: different times
- **иногда**: sometimes
- **ссорились**: quarreled
- **мало денег**: little money
- **делали ошибки**: made mistakes
- **самая главная вещь**: the most important thing
- **любовь**: love
- **решать**: solve
- **проблемы**: problems
- **например**: for example
- **около двух лет**: for about two years
- **безработным**: unemployed
- **бы**: would (subjunctive mood)
- **обычная женщина**: usual woman
- **найди работу**: find a job (imperative)
- **кормить**: feed
- **жаловалась**: complained
- **не навсегда**: not forever
- **права**: right
- **написал книгу**: wrote a book
- **стала**: became
- **популярной**: popular
- **писателем**: writer (ablative)
- **вдохновения**: inspiration (genitive)
- **опять**: again
- **поддерживала**: supported
- **ещё один пример**: one more example
- **тридцать пять**: thirty five
- **плохо себя чувствовала**: felt unwell
- **рак**: cancer
- **боролись**: fought
- **пять**: five
- **победили**: won
- **короче говоря**: long story short
- **жизнь**: life
- **благодаря**: thanks to
- **история**: story
- **встретились**: met

11

- **обожаем**: adore
- **рассказывать**: tell
- **многие**: many people
- **верят**: believe
- **итак**: so
- **девятнадцать**: nineteen
- **поступил**: entered
- **в Париже**: in Paris
- **в общежитии**: in the dormitory
- **мечтал**: dreamed
- **богатым**: rich
- **тогда**: then
- **что это**: that it is
- **сразу заметил**: noticed at once
- **отличалась от**: was different from
- **девушек**: girls (genitive)
- **оказалось**: turned out
- **студентка по обмену**: an exchange student
- **из России**: from Russia
- **на год**: for a year
- **легко**: easily
- **общаться**: communicate
- **показал**: showed
- **город**: city
- **познакомил**: introduced
- **понимали друг друга**: understood each other
- **романтические чувства**: romantic feelings
- **странно**: strangely
- **в начале**: in the beginning
- **через полгода**: in half a year
- **может**: maybe
- **начали встречаться**: started dating
- **здорово**: great
- **долгие**: long
- **поцелуи**: kisses
- **стихи**: poems
- **уедет**: will leave
- **не могла**: couldn't
- **остаться**: stay
- **если**: if
- **женишься**: will marry
- **сможет**: will be able
- **только**: only
- **удивительная**: amazing
- **другие**: other
- **а что если**: and what if
- **судьба**: destiny
- **в чём проблема**: what's the problem
- **теперь**: now
- **боялся ответственности**: was afraid of responsibility
- **потерять свободу**: lose freedom

- **не сделал предложение**: didn't propose
- **обменялись адресами**: exchanged addresses
- **пиши**: write (imperative)
- **обещай**: promise (imperative)
- **несколько**: a few
- **учёба**: studies
- **не забыл**: didn't forget
- **заставил себя**: made myself
- **не поедешь**: won't go
- **во Францию**: to France
- **молодой**: young
- **лучше**: better
- **огромная**: huge
- **прошло три года**: three years passed
- **сравнивал**: compared
- **лучшая**: the best
- **так поздно**: so late
- **извинюсь**: will apologize
- **умолять**: beg
- **простит**: will forgive
- **брошу**: will give up
- **попросишь**: will ask
- **переехать**: move
- **это не важно**: it doesn't matter
- **в Антарктиде**: in Antarctica
- **длинное письмо**: a long letter
- **хранит**: keeps
- **получила**: received
- **через пять лет**: in five years
- **сменила**: changed
- **вернулось**: came back
- **как**: how
- **найти**: find
- **фамилию**: surname (accusative)
- **сколько**: how many
- **в другой стране**: in another country
- **семьи**: families
- **уверен**: sure
- **вышла замуж**: got married (only about women)
- **одинок**: single
- **свидание вслепую**: a blind date
- **почему нет**: why not
- **немного опоздал**: was a bit late
- **уже**: already
- **пришла**: came
- **голову**: head (accusative)

- **спину**: back (accusative)
- **сразу узнал**: recognized at once

- **как**: how
- **другая история**: a different story

Questions about the story

1. **Когда Серж был безработным, Лена...**
   When Serge was unemployed, Lena...

   a. Говорила ему найти работу.
      Told him to find a job.

   b. Не любила его.
      Didn't love him.

   c. Поддерживала его.
      Supported him.

   d. Жаловалась.
      Complained.

2. **Серж и Лена начали встречаться через...**
   Serge and Lena began to date in...

   a. 6 месяцев.
      6 months.

   b. Три года.
      Three years.

   c. Пять лет.
      Five years.

   d. Год.
      A year.

3. **Почему Серж не сделал Лене предложение?**
   Why didn't Serge propose to Lena?

   a. Он не любил её.
      He didn't love her.

   b. Он боялся ответственности.
      He was afraid of responsibility.

c. Он нашёл другую девушку.
He found another girl.

d. Его друг посоветовал ему не жениться на ней.
His friend advised him not to marry her.

4. **Лена вышла замуж за другого мужчину. Правда или ложь?**
Lena married another man. True or false?

a. Правда.
True.

b. Ложь.
False.

5. **Где Серж встретил Лену через восемь лет?**
Where did Serge meet Lena in eight years?

a. России.
In Russia.

b. В университете.
At the University.

c. На свидании вслепую.
On a blind date.

d. На улице.
In the street.

Answers

1. C
2. A
3. B
4. B
5. C

CHAPTER II

Идеальный писатель —
A Perfect Writer

Я люблю **читать книги**. Я **много** читал **в детстве**. Я любил **литературу** в школе. **Учительница** часто **хвалила** меня. Я писал хорошие **сочинения**. **Друзья** всегда **просили помочь** им с **домашним заданием**.

Время прошло. Я **вырос**. **Но** я **всё равно** люблю читать. Мне нравится **разная** литература. **Сказки, романы, фантастика, приключения, короткие рассказы** и **даже ужасы**. У меня нет **любимого писателя**. Очень **тяжело выбрать**.

Я **больше** люблю **печатные** книги. **Электронные книги удобны**, но это **не для меня**. **Каждый месяц** я покупаю **несколько книг**. **За углом** есть **книжный магазин**. У них **большой выбор**. Я **долго выбираю** книги. Я **интересуюсь** разными книгами. Есть хорошие **современные** книги.

К сожалению, книги **дорого стоят**. **Поэтому я беру** их у друзей. Нам нравится **обсуждать** книги. **Чаще всего мы собираемся на выходных**.

Недавно моя **подруга** сказала мне **одну вещь**. Я **удивился**.

— **Игорь**, тебе **всегда что-нибудь** не нравится. Ты **видишь слишком много минусов. Зачем** ты покупаешь книги? Зачем ты их читаешь?

— **Извини, Света**. Я **уверен**, можно **написать лучше**. Да, я люблю книги. Но в **каждой** есть минусы.

— **Отлично**. Ты любишь книги. **Напиши** книгу или рассказ **сам**. **Без** минусов.

— **Нет проблем**. Я **сделаю** это **к следующей субботе**. **Согласна**?

— **Конечно**. Я **буду ждать**, идеальный писатель.

У меня была **неделя**. Я **не спешил**. Написать рассказ? Я так много их прочитал. Я **справлюсь**. **Не переживай**. Я **вспомнил** школьные сочинения. Я **знал**, что у меня есть **талант**.

Неделя прошла **быстро**. Я **вспомнил** о рассказе **в пятницу**. **Никакой паники! Всё будет хорошо**. Я **сел за стол**. **Взял ручку**, листок **бумаги**. Сделал **крепкий кофе**. Прошло 20 **минут, час, два**... Я посмотрел на **часы**. О нет! Я не мог **поверить**. **Может быть**, часы **сломаны**? Я **посмотрел в окно**. **Пустые улицы. Темнота. Ночь**.

Я был **зол**. Я **понял**, что быть **писателем** тяжело. У меня не было **идей**. Я **устал** и хотел **спать**. Я **выпил** кофе, но это не помогло.

Я **проснулся. Звонил телефон**. Это была Света.

— **Давай встретимся вечером**, идеальный писатель.

— Да, **где** и **во сколько**?

— **В кафе, в шесть**.

— **Хорошо**.

— **До встречи**, Игорь.

У меня было **плохое настроение**. Я **выкинул** листок бумаги. Я не хотел идти в кафе. Я **принял душ** и **успокоился**. Я **обещал** — я пойду.

— **Привет**, Игорь.

— Привет, Света.

— **Мне не терпится послушать** твой рассказ.

— Я хорошо его помню. **Сейчас расскажу**.

— Я **внимательно** слушаю.

— **Жил-был мальчик**. **Его звали** Игорь. Он любил книги и много читал. У него была **умная** подруга. Её звали Света. Они **вместе** обсуждали книги. Но Игорь всегда **искал** минусы. Он умел писать лучше. Он **так думал**. Тогда Света **попросила** его написать рассказ. Идеальный. Без минусов. Он согласился. Он не знал, что это очень трудно. **Ничего не вышло**. Сейчас он сидит в кафе со своей подругой Светой. Она **дала** ему хороший **урок**. Он **ей благодарен**. Он хочет искать **плюсы**.

Света **смеялась**. У меня было **отличное** настроение.

Краткое содержание истории

Игорь любит читать книги. Он любил читать в школе и писал хорошие сочинения. Время прошло, но он всё равно любит читать. Он обсуждает книги со своей подругой Светой. Но он всегда ищет минусы. Так сказала Света. Она попросила его написать идеальный рассказ. Без минусов. Игорь согласился. Он был уверен, что всё будет хорошо. Но это было трудно. Ничего не вышло. Он встретился со Светой и рассказал историю. История была о нём и о Свете. Он благодарен Свете. Она дала ему хороший урок: писателем быть трудно.

Summary of the story

Igor enjoys reading books. He liked reading at school and wrote great essays. The time has passed, but he still likes reading. He discusses books with his friend Sveta. But he's always looking for disadvantages. Sveta said so. She asked him to write a perfect story. Without disadvantages. Igor agreed. He was sure everything would be ok. But that was hard to do. It didn't work out. He met Sveta and told a story. That was a story about him and Sveta. He's grateful to Sveta. She taught him a good lesson — it's hard to be a writer.

Vocabulary

- **идеальный**: perfect
- **писатель**: writer
- **читать книги**: read books
- **много**: a lot
- **в детстве**: as a child
- **литературу**: literature (accusative)
- **учительница**: teacher (female)
- **хвалила**: praised
- **сочинения**: essays
- **друзья**: friends
- **просили помочь**: asked for help
- **домашним заданием**: homework (ablative)
- **время прошло**: time passed
- **вырос**: grew up
- **но**: but
- **всё равно**: all the same
- **разная**: different
- **сказки**: fairy tales
- **романы**: novels
- **фантастика**: science fiction
- **приключения**: adventures
- **короткие рассказы**: short stories
- **даже ужасы**: even horrors
- **любимого писателя**: favorite writer (genitive)
- **тяжело выбрать**: hard to choose
- **больше**: more
- **печатные**: printed
- **электронные книги**: e-books
- **удобны**: handy (short form)
- **не для меня**: not for me
- **каждый месяц**: every month
- **несколько книг**: several books
- **за углом**: round the corner
- **книжный магазин**: bookshop
- **большой выбор**: wide range
- **долго выбираю**: choose for a long time
- **интересуюсь**: interested in
- **современные**: modern
- **к сожалению**: unfortunately

- **дорого стоят**: are expensive
- **поэтому**: that's why
- **беру их у друзей**: take them from friends
- **обсуждать**: discuss
- **чаще всего**: most often
- **собираемся на выходных**: meet on the weekend
- **недавно**: recently
- **подруга**: friend (female)
- **одну вещь**: one thing
- **удивился**: was surprised
- **Игорь**: Igor
- **всегда**: always
- **что-нибудь**: something
- **видишь**: see
- **слишком много минусов**: too many disadvantages
- **зачем**: why
- **извини**: sorry
- **Света**: Sveta
- **уверен**: sure
- **написать лучше**: write better
- **каждой**: each
- **отлично**: great
- **напиши**: write (imperative)
- **сам**: yourself
- **без**: without
- **нет проблем**: no problem
- **сделаю**: will do
- **к следующей субботе**: by next Saturday
- **согласна**: agree
- **конечно**: of course
- **буду ждать**: will be waiting
- **неделя**: week
- **не спешил**: didn't hurry
- **справлюсь**: will manage
- **не переживай**: don't worry (imperative)
- **вспомнил**: remembered
- **знал**: knew
- **талант**: talent
- **быстро**: quickly
- **в пятницу**: on Friday
- **никакой паники**: no panic
- **всё будет хорошо**: everything's going to be ok
- **сел за стол**: sat down at the table
- **взял ручку**: took a pen
- **бумаги**: paper (genitive)
- **крепкий кофе**: strong coffee
- **минут**: minutes (genitive)
- **час**: hour

- **два**: two
- **часы**: clock
- **поверить**: believe
- **может быть**: maybe
- **сломаны**: broken
- **посмотрел в окно**: looked out the window
- **пустые улицы**: empty streets
- **темнота**: darkness
- **ночь**: night
- **зол**: angry (short form)
- **понял**: understood
- **идей**: ideas (plural genitive)
- **устал**: was tired
- **спать**: sleep
- **выпил**: drank
- **проснулся**: woke up
- **звонил телефон**: the phone was ringing
- **давай встретимся вечером**: let's meet in the evening
- **где**: where
- **во сколько**: at what time
- **в кафе**: at the cafe
- **в шесть**: at six
- **хорошо**: ok
- **до встречи**: see you
- **плохое настроение**: bad mood
- **выкинул**: threw out
- **принял душ**: took a shower
- **успокоился**: calmed down
- **обещал**: promised
- **привет**: hello
- **мне не терпится послушать**: I can't wait to hear
- **сейчас расскажу**: now I'll tell
- **внимательно**: attentively
- **жил-был мальчик**: once upon a time there lived a boy
- **его звали**: his name was
- **умная**: smart
- **вместе**: together
- **искал**: looked for
- **так думал**: thought so
- **попросила**: asked
- **ничего не вышло**: it didn't work out
- **дала урок**: taught a lesson
- **ей благодарен**: grateful to her
- **плюсы**: advantages
- **смеялась**: laughed
- **отличное**: excellent

Questions about the story

1. **Игорь любит читать книги. Но в школе не любил читать. Правда или ложь?**
   Igor likes reading. But he didn't like reading at school. True or false?

   a. Правда.
      True.

   b. Ложь.
      False.

2. **Игорю не нравятся современные книги. Правда или ложь?**
   Igor doesn't like modern books. True or false?

   a. Правда.
      True.

   b. Ложь.
      False.

3. **О чём подруга попросила Игоря?**
   What did Igor's friend ask him to do?

   a. Написать сочинение.
      Write an essay.

   b. Написать стихотворение.
      Write a poem.

   c. Написать роман.
      Write a novel.

   d. Написать рассказ.
      Write a story.

4. **Игорь понял: быть писателем...**
   Igor understood: being a writer is...

   a. Легко.
      Easy.

   b. Интересно.
      Interesting.

   c. Трудно.
      Hard.

   d. Неинтересно.
      Not interesting.

5. **Что делала Света в конце истории?**
   What was Sveta doing at the end of the story?

   a. Смеялась.
      Laughing.

   b. Кричала.
      Shouting.

   c. Плакала.
      Crying.

   d. Пила кофе.
      Drinking coffee.

Answers

1. B
2. B
3. D
4. C
5. A

CHAPTER III

Спасатели — Rescuers

Меня зовут Виктор. Мне **пятьдесят пять** лет. Я **всегда хотел** быть **врачом**. И я всегда знал, что я хочу **лечить** детей. Я хочу **спасать жизни**. Я **получил** хорошее **образование**. Я работаю с **новорождёнными** детьми. **Это здорово**! Но это очень **сложно**. **В конце концов**, я не **Бог**. Иногда я **ничего** не могу сделать.

Двадцать пять лет назад у меня был **особенный пациент**. Я не буду объяснять **детали**. Я скажу **одно**. Все мои **коллеги** говорили:

— Ты не спасёшь его. Это **невозможно**. **Прими** это. Он **умрёт**. **Может**, сегодня или завтра.

Но я **не мог сидеть** и **смотреть**, как он умирает. Я не мог смотреть, как **плачут** его **родители**. Я сказал им:

— Я ничего не **обещаю**. Это очень **сложный случай**. У меня **большой опыт**, но я не **волшебник**.

Что они могли **ответить**? Они были **готовы на всё**. Я **провёл** в **больнице** около **недели**. Я не ездил домой. Я не видел свою семью. Я **мало спал**. Но у меня была **надежда**. Я работал и **молился**. **Прошло два дня**, а **малыш** был **жив**. Прошло четыре дня, и его **состояние не ухудшилось**. **Через** неделю **ему стало лучше**. Мои коллеги **поверили в** меня. Мы спасли малыша. Он провёл в больнице **больше трёх месяцев**. Но он был жив. Я **запомнил** этого мальчика и его семью **на всю жизнь**.

Около месяца назад я **поехал в отпуск**. Моя **жена** и **сыновья** уже **ждали** меня **на побережье**. **Погода** была **прекрасной**. Я **любовался природой**. Обычно я очень **внимательный водитель**, но… **Неожиданно на встречной полосе появилась** машина. «**Действуй быстро**», — подумал я.

Я повернул **руль, секунда**… **Что происходит? Почему** я вижу деревья **вверх ногами**? Моя машина **перевернулась**. **Слава Богу**, мой **мобильный** был **близко**. Я **вызвал спасателей**. Я **отстегнул ремень** и перевернулся. **Затем** я попытался **открыть** дверь. **Бесполезно. Через пару минут** машина была **в огне. Дым**, огонь! Я **задыхался. Вскоре** я увидел спасателей. Они **прибыли** быстро.

«**Я спасён**», — подумал я **с облегчением. Пять** или **шесть ребят** вышли из машины. Но почему они **ничего не делают**? Почему не спасают меня? Они **стояли и смотрели! Никто** не хотел **рисковать жизнью. «Неужели** это **конец**?!» — подумал я **в ужасе**. Но что это? Какой-то **молодой человек** побежал **вперёд. Только** один! Я **потерял сознание**.

Я **пришёл в себя** и **оглянулся**. Я жив. Я в больнице. Вот моя жена. Я **позвал** её. **Несколько минут** мы просто **плакали**. Потом пришли наши **сыновья**. Я **рассказал** им **всё**.

— Я **помню**: те ребята стояли и смотрели. Я не **виню** их. Машина была в огне. Они могли умереть. Но я хочу **знать, кто** спас меня.

— Я думаю, это можно **узнать**, — сказала моя жена. — Я **позвоню** им.

Она **набрала номер, описала** мой случай, **задала вопрос, поблагодарила** и **повесила трубку**. Затем она назвала **имя и фамилию** молодого человека.

— **Что не так**, папа? Почему ты **такой бледный**? — спросил мой **старший** сын.

— Я **должен** его увидеть, — ответил я.

Я быстро **поправился**. Я не поехал домой. Я узнал **адрес** того спасателя. Я **постучал в дверь**. **На пороге** стояла женщина. Я **сразу узнал** её. Она узнала меня. **Много лет назад** я спас её сына. **Совсем недавно** он спас меня...

Краткое содержание истории

Виктор — врач. Около двадцати пяти лет назад он вылечил маленького мальчика. Все его коллеги сказали, что ребёнка спасти невозможно. Но Виктор не мог смотреть, как он умирает. Ему удалось спасти малыша.

Несколько месяцев назад Виктор попал в автокатастрофу. Он не мог открыть дверь. Виктор вызвал спасателей. Они прибыли довольно быстро. Машина была вся в огне. Но никто не хотел рисковать своей жизнью. Только один из спасателей оказался достаточно храбрым, чтобы спасти Виктора.

Вскоре Виктор поправился, узнал адрес спасателя и навестил его. Оказалось, что его спас мальчик, которого Виктор вылечил двадцать пять лет назад.

Summary of the story

Victor is a doctor. About twenty five years ago, he cured a little boy. All his colleagues said it was impossible to save him. But Victor couldn't watch him die. He managed to save the baby.

A few months ago, Victor got in a car crash. He couldn't open the door. Victor called the rescue team. They arrived quite quickly. The whole car was on fire. But nobody wanted to risk their lives. Only one of them turned out to be brave enough to save Victor.

Victor recovered soon and found out the rescuer's address and visited him. It turned out Victor was saved by the boy he had cured twenty five years ago.

Vocabulary

- **спасатели**: rescuers
- **пятьдесят пять**: fifty five
- **всегда хотел**: has always wanted
- **врачом**: doctor (ablative)
- **лечить**: cure
- **спасать жизни**: save lives
- **получил**: got
- **образование**: education
- **новорожденными**: newborn
- **это здорово**: it's great
- **сложно**: hard
- **в конце концов**: after all
- **Бог**: God
- **иногда**: sometimes
- **ничего**: nothing
- **двадцать пять лет назад**: twenty five years ago
- **особенный пациент**: special patient
- **детали**: details
- **одно**: one thing
- **коллеги**: colleagues
- **невозможно**: impossible
- **прими**: accept (imperative)
- **умрёт**: will die
- **может**: maybe
- **не мог**: couldn't
- **сидеть**: sit
- **смотреть**: watch
- **плачут**: cry
- **родители**: parents
- **обещаю**: promise
- **сложный случай**: complicated case
- **большой опыт**: extensive experience
- **волшебник**: magician
- **ответить**: reply
- **готовы на всё**: ready for everything
- **провёл**: spent
- **в больнице**: in hospital
- **недели**: week (genitive)
- **мало спал**: had little sleep
- **надежда**: hope
- **молился**: was praying
- **прошло два дня**: two days passed
- **малыш**: baby
- **жив**: alive
- **состояние**: condition
- **не ухудшилось**: didn't get worse
- **через**: in (in a period of time)

- **ему стало лучше**: he got better
- **поверили в**: believed in
- **больше трёх месяцев**: more than three months
- **запомнил**: remembered
- **на всю жизнь**: for life
- **поехал в отпуск**: went on holiday
- **жена**: wife
- **сыновья**: sons
- **ждали**: were waiting
- **на побережье**: at the seaside
- **погода**: weather
- **прекрасной**: wonderful
- **любовался природой**: was admiring nature
- **внимательный водитель**: attentive driver
- **неожиданно**: unexpectedly
- **на встречной полосе**: on the opposite lane
- **появилась**: appeared
- **действуй быстро**: act fast (imperative)
- **руль**: steering wheel
- **секунда**: second
- **что происходит**: what's going on
- **почему**: why
- **вверх ногами**: upside down
- **перевернулась**: turned over
- **слава Богу**: thanks God
- **мобильный**: mobile
- **близко**: close
- **вызвал спасателей**: called the rescuers
- **отстегнул ремень**: unbuckled
- **затем**: then
- **открыть**: open
- **бесполезно**: no use
- **через пару минут**: in a couple of minutes
- **в огне**: on fire
- **дым**: smoke
- **задыхался**: was choking
- **вскоре**: soon
- **прибыли**: arrived
- **я спасён**: I'm saved
- **с облегчением**: with relief
- **пять**: five
- **шесть**: six
- **ребят**: guys (genitive)
- **ничего не делают**: don't do anything
- **стояли и смотрели**: were standing and watching

- **никто**: nobody
- **рисковать жизнью**: risk life
- **неужели**: really
- **конец**: end
- **в ужасе**: in horror
- **молодой человек**: young man
- **вперёд**: ahead
- **только**: only
- **потерял сознание**: lost consciousness
- **пришёл в себя**: came round
- **оглянулся**: looked around
- **позвал**: called
- **несколько минут**: for a few minutes
- **плакали**: were crying
- **сыновья**: sons
- **рассказал**: told
- **всё**: everything
- **помню**: remember
- **виню**: blame
- **знать, кто**: know who
- **узнать**: find out

- **позвоню**: will call
- **набрала номер**: dialed the number
- **описала**: described
- **задала вопрос**: asked the question
- **поблагодарила**: thanked
- **повесила трубку**: hung up
- **имя и фамилию**: name and surname
- **что не так**: what's wrong
- **такой бледный**: so pale
- **старший**: elder
- **должен**: must
- **поправился**: recovered
- **адрес**: address
- **постучал в дверь**: knocked on the door
- **на пороге**: at the doorstep
- **сразу узнал**: recognized at once
- **много лет назад**: many years ago
- **совсем недавно**: just recently

Questions about the story

1. **Виктор думает, что он может спасти всех. Правда или ложь?**
   Victor thinks he can save everyone. True or false?

   a. Правда.
      True.

   b. Ложь.
      False.

2. **Сколько лет назад у него был особенный пациент?**
   How many years ago did Victor have a special patient?

   a. 52.
   b. 25.
   c. 55.
   d. 3.

3. **Куда ехал Виктор, когда его машина перевернулась?**
   Where was Victor going when his car turned over?

   a. В отпуск.
      On holiday.

   b. На работу.
      To work.

   c. На пикник.
      On a picnic.

   d. В магазин.
      To the shop.

4. **Спасатели не хотели рисковать жизнью. Правда или ложь?**
   The rescuers didn't want to risk their lives. True or false?

   a. Правда.
      True.

   b. Ложь.
      False.

5. **Кто спас Виктора?**
   Who saved Victor?

   a. Спасатели.
      Rescuers.

   b. Его жена.
      His wife.

   c. Мальчик, которого спас Виктор.
      The boy Victor saved.

   d. Его старший сын.
      His elder son.

Answers

1. B
2. B
3. A
4. A
5. C

CHAPTER IV

Подарок — A Present

Я не **люблю** спорт. Бег, плавание, **отжимания** — всё это не **для меня**. Я не **активный человек**. Я люблю **проводить время дома**. Я **часто смотрю** фильмы, читаю книги, готовлю, играю **на гитаре**. Иногда встречаюсь с **друзьями**. Мы **общаемся**, играем в **настольные игры**, **шутим**, делимся новостями.

Совсем забыл: у меня **лишний вес**. Да, я **толстый**. **Точнее**, я **был** толстым.

Однажды всё изменилось. У меня **очень хорошие** друзья. Они **всегда** меня **поддерживали**. **Два года назад** у меня был **день рождения**. Я не **хотел отмечать**. **Зачем**?

За неделю до дня рождения я встретился с другом.

— Ты хочешь измениться, **Дима**? — **спросил** он.

— Да, **Саша**, очень. Но **ничего не выходит**. Спорт — это не для меня.

— Я **не только о** весе. И о **настроении тоже**.

— Ты **можешь помочь**?

— Да. Я **сделаю** тебе **классный подарок**. Это хорошее **лекарство от** лишнего веса и **грусти**.

— **Тогда приглашаю** тебя на **вечеринку через** неделю.

— **Хорошо**.

Это было **интересно**. Я **никогда не пробовал такие лекарства**. У меня была **надежда**.

В день моего рождения мы устроили вечеринку. Праздновали дома: я не люблю **кафе** и **рестораны**. Было **весело**. **Много шариков, пицца, кола. Пришло время** дарить подарки. Их было много. Книги, **билет** на **концерт, несколько** настольных игр. Мне всё понравилось. Мои друзья хорошо меня **знают**. Саша дарил **последним**. Я **волновался**. Саша **дал** мне **большую коробку**. Я **удивился**. Такая коробка? Для лекарства? Я **начал открывать** подарок... Я **был в шоке**! Не **мог поверить**! В коробке был **маленький щенок**.

— **Нужно** дать ей **имя**! Это **девочка**, — **сказали** друзья.
— Надежда — хорошее имя, — сказал Саша.
— **Отлично**, — **ответил** я.

Мне было всё равно. Я так **долго** ждал. И что **теперь**? Лекарство, **конечно**. Мне было очень **грустно**. Саша это **заметил**.

— Ты **поймёшь**. Поверь мне. Это хорошее лекарство, — сказал он.

На **следующее утро** я **рано встал**. Надежда **запрыгнула** на **кровать**. Она **хотела играть**. Я хотел **спать**. Вечеринка **поздно закончилась**. У меня не было **выбора**. Я встал, **умылся, почистил зубы, причесался**. Мы **вышли на улицу**. Я **достал телефон** и **сделал фото**. Было **красивое осеннее** утро. Надежда **быстро бегала**. Щенок **кусал листья** и **смешно гавкал**. Я **улыбнулся**.

Через час мы **вернулись** домой. Я начал есть пиццу. Надежда **смотрела** на меня. Она **положила лапу** мне на **руку**.

— Ты **тоже** хочешь есть? — спросил я.
— **Гав**! — ответила Надежда.

Я **отложил** пиццу, **взял кастрюлю, налил немного воды**. Я приготовил **овсянку** с **курицей**. Я любил готовить. **Но я редко** готовил не **для себя**. Это было интересно. И **вкусно**. Она **заснула** у меня на руках. **Собака** была **такой милой**!

Я **посчитал**: **за один день** мы гуляли **три** часа. **Трудно представить**!

Через неделю я встретился с Сашей.

— Это ты, Дима? — спросил мой друг.
— Конечно. **Почему** ты спрашиваешь?
— Ты изменился. Эта **рубашка** тебе **большая**.
— **Правда**?
— Надежда — хорошее лекарство.

Я **не только сбросил** вес. Я **нашёл** друга. Мы **никогда** не **скучаем**. **Спасибо** Саше **за** лекарство.

Краткое содержание истории

Я не люблю спорт. Я не активный человек. Я люблю встречаться друзьями, готовить, смотреть фильмы. У меня был лишний вес. Я не хотел отмечать свой день рождения. Но мой друг Саша хотел подарить мне лекарство. Это был щенок по имени Надежда. Я удивился. Саша попросил поверить ему: это поможет. Я много гулял со щенком, готовил ему и веселился. Я не только сбросил вес. Я нашёл друга. Спасибо за лекарство, Саша.

Summary of the story

I don't like sports. I'm not an active person. I like meeting friends, cooking, watching films. I was overweight. I didn't feel like celebrating my birthday. But my friend Sasha wanted to give me a cure. That was a puppy named Hope. I was surprised. Sasha asked to believe him: that would help. I walked a lot with the puppy, cooked for it and had fun. I didn't just lose weight. I found a friend. Thanks for the cure, Sasha.

Vocabulary

- **люблю спорт**: love sports
- **бег**: running
- **плавание**: swimming
- **отжимания**: push-ups
- **для меня**: for me
- **активный человек**: active person
- **проводить время дома**: spend time at home
- **часто**: often
- **смотрю фильмы**: watch films
- **читаю книги**: read books
- **готовлю**: cook
- **играю на гитаре**: play the guitar
- **иногда**: sometimes
- **встречаюсь**: meet
- **друзьями**: friends (ablative)
- **общаемся**: talk
- **настольные игры**: board games
- **шутим**: make jokes
- **делимся новостями**: share news
- **совсем забыл**: completely forgot
- **лишний вес**: extra weight
- **толстый**: fat
- **точнее**: to be more exact
- **был**: was
- **однажды**: one day
- **изменилось**: changed
- **очень хорошие**: very good
- **всегда**: always
- **поддерживали**: supported
- **два года назад**: two years ago
- **день рождения**: birthday
- **хотел отмечать**: wanted to celebrate
- **зачем**: what for
- **за неделю до**: week before
- **Дима**: Dima
- **спросил**: asked
- **Саша**: Sasha
- **ничего не выходит**: nothing works out
- **не только о**: not only about
- **настроении**: mood (prepositional)
- **тоже**: too
- **можешь**: can

- **помочь**: help
- **сделаю**: will make
- **классный**: cool
- **подарок**: present
- **лекарство от**: cure for
- **грусти**: sadness (genitive)
- **тогда**: then
- **приглашаю**: invite
- **вечеринку**: party (accusative)
- **через**: in (about time)
- **хорошо**: ok
- **интересно**: interesting
- **никогда не пробовал такие лекарства**: have never tried such medicines
- **надежда**: hope
- **кафе**: cafes
- **рестораны**: restaurants
- **весело**: fun
- **много**: a lot
- **шариков**: balloons (genitive)
- **пицца**: pizza
- **кола**: cola
- **пришло время**: time has come
- **билет**: ticket
- **концерт**: concert
- **несколько**: several
- **знают**: know
- **последним**: last
- **волновался**: was worried
- **дал**: gave
- **большую коробку**: big box (accusative)
- **удивился**: was surprised
- **начал открывать**: began to open
- **был в шоке**: was shocked
- **мог поверить**: could believe
- **маленький щенок**: little puppy
- **нужно**: need
- **имя**: name
- **девочка**: girl
- **сказали**: said
- **отлично**: great
- **ответил**: answered
- **мне было всё равно**: it didn't matter to me
- **долго**: for a long time
- **теперь**: now
- **конечно**: of course
- **грустно**: sad
- **заметил**: noticed
- **поймёшь**: will understand
- **следующее утро**: next morning
- **рано встал**: woke up early
- **запрыгнула**: jumped

- **кровать**: bed
- **хотела**: wanted
- **играть**: play
- **спать**: sleep
- **поздно закончилась**: ended late
- **выбора**: choice (genitive)
- **умылся**: washed my face
- **почистил зубы**: brushed teeth
- **причесался**: brushed hair
- **вышли на улицу**: went outside
- **достал телефон**: got the phone
- **сделал фото**: take a photo
- **красивое**: beautiful
- **осеннее**: autumn
- **быстро бегала**: ran fast
- **кусал листья**: bit leaves
- **смешно**: funny
- **гавкал**: barked
- **улыбнулся**: smiled
- **через час**: in an hour
- **вернулись**: came back
- **смотрела**: looked
- **положила лапу**: put the paw
- **руку**: hand (accusative)
- **тоже**: too
- **гав**: woof
- **отложил**: put away
- **взял кастрюлю**: took a pot
- **налил немного воды**: poured some water
- **овсянку**: oatmeal (accusative)
- **курицей**: chicken (ablative)
- **но**: but
- **редко**: rarely
- **для себя**: for myself
- **вкусно**: tasty
- **заснула**: fell asleep
- **собака**: dog
- **такой милой**: so cute
- **посчитал**: counted
- **за один день**: in a day
- **три**: three
- **трудно представить**: hard to imagine
- **почему**: why
- **рубашка**: shirt
- **большая**: loose
- **правда**: really
- **не только сбросил**: not only lost
- **нашёл**: found
- **никогда**: never
- **скучаем**: are bored
- **спасибо за**: thanks for

Questions about the story

1. Дима часто читает...
   Dima often reads...

   a. Журналы.
      Magazines.

   b. Газеты.
      Newspapers.

   c. Книги.
      Books.

   d. Комиксы.
      Comics.

2. Дима хотел отметить свой день рождения. Правда или ложь?
   Dima wanted to celebrate his birthday. True or false?

   a. Правда.
      True.

   b. Ложь.
      False.

3. Саша подарил Диме...
   Sasha gave Dima...

   a. Интерес.
      Interest.

   b. Дружбу.
      Friendship.

   c. Любовь.
      Love.

d. Надежду.
Hope.

4. **Как долго Дима гулял со щенком?**
   How long has Dima been walking the puppy?

   a. Три минуты.
   Three minutes.

   b. Три часа.
   Three hours.

   c. Два часа.
   Two hours.

   d. Три дня.
   Three days.

5. **Кого нашёл Дима?**
   Whom has Dima found?

   a. Друга.
   A friend.

   b. Сашу.
   Sasha

   c. Пиццу.
   A pizza.

   d. Котёнка.
   A kitten.

Answers

1. C
2. B
3. D
4. B
5. A

CHAPTER V

Менделеев — Mendeleev

Вы любите **химию**? Вы любите **формулы**? **Даже если нет**, вы слышали про **таблицу Менделеева**. Её **изобрёл учёный** по **фамилии** Менделеев. Хотите **узнать** о нём? **Читайте дальше**.

Его **полное** имя — **Дмитрий Иванович** Менделеев. Иванович — это **отчество**. Это **значит**, его **отца** звали Иван.

Дмитрий **родился в середине девятнадцатого века**. Его отец был **директором гимназии**. Его мать была **домохозяйкой**. **Только представьте**: в семье было **семнадцать детей**! **Великий химик** был **последним**.

Его отец **умер**, когда Дмитрий был **маленьким мальчиком**. Его мать Мария **вырастила** его **одна**. У Дмитрия было **отличное образование**.

Менделеев был **не только** химиком. Он работал **в сельском хозяйстве** и **промышленности**. Он даже **конструировал корабли** и **воздушные шары**!

А что насчёт личной жизни? Менделеев **был женат дважды**. Его первая жена была **на восемь лет его старше**. У них было **трое детей**. Когда ему было **сорок два**, Менделеев **влюбился в** другую **женщину**. Или девушку? Ей было **всего шестнадцать**! Она **родила** ему **четырёх** детей. **Удивительно**, но сегодня у учёного нет **ни одного потомка**.

Есть **несколько мифов** о Менделееве. **Говорят**, что он **увидел** свою **знаменитую** таблицу **во сне**. Это **не правда**. Он **думал** о ней **двадцать лет**. **Однажды** ему **рассказали** об этом мифе. Учёный очень **расстроился**. Это был **огромный труд**. Другой миф: Менделеев **изобрёл водку**. **Снова ложь**. Это **было сделано до него**.

Что любил великий учёный? Он **обожал классическую музыку**. **Особенно** Бетховена. Он **также** любил **делать что-нибудь своими руками**. Например, **чемоданы**. **В старости** он был **полностью слепым**. Но **продолжал** делать **такие вещи**. Он часто **играл в шахматы**. А ещё он часто ходил **в баню** — **русскую сауну**. Менделеев любил **чай**. Но только чай **по рецепту** его жены.

Дмитрий Иванович был **толерантным человеком**. Он **читал лекции** для женщин. Не **удивительно**? **Для нашего времени**. Тогда женщины **не могли** получить **высшее образование**. Менделеев **ненавидел расизм** и любил **свободу**.

У Менделеева есть **Нобелевская премия**? Нет! Несколько **номинаций**, но премии нет. Говорят, у него был **конфликт с братьями** Нобелями.

И наконец, парадокс: великий химик **не признавал медицину**! Он **не обращался к врачам**. У учёного было **отличное здоровье**. Он **прожил семьдесят два года**. **Причина** смерти — **воспаление лёгких**.

Краткое содержание истории

Эта история — краткая биография Дмитрия Ивановича Менделеева. Он русский учёный. Он создал таблицу химических элементов. Он родился в середине девятнадцатого века. Он был младшим из семнадцати детей. Его отец умер, когда Менделеев был маленьким мальчиком.

У учёного было хорошее образование. Он работал в разных сферах: химия, промышленность и сельское хозяйство.

Менделеев был женат два раза. Есть несколько мифов о нём. Говорят, что он изобрёл водку и увидел свою таблицу во сне. Это неправда.

Он любил классическую музыку и шахматы. Он также любил делать вещи своими руками. Например, чемоданы. В старости он был полностью слепым.

Менделеев читал лекции для женщин, ненавидел расизм. Он любил свободу. У учёного не было Нобелевской премии. Он прожил семьдесят два года и умер от воспаления лёгких.

Summary of the story

This story is a short biography of Dmitry Ivanovich Mendeleev. He's a Russian scientist. He created the table of chemical elements. He was born in the middle of the nineteenth century. He was the youngest among seventeen children. His father died when Mendeleev was a little boy.

The scientist had a good education. He worked in various spheres: chemistry, industry and agriculture.

Mendeleev was married two times. There are several myths about him. They say he invented vodka and saw his table in a dream. It's not true.He liked classical music and chess. He also liked making things with his own hands. For example, suitcases. In the old age, he was completely blind.

Mendeleev gave lectures to women and hated racism. He loved freedom. The scientist didn't have a Nobel prize. He lived seventy two years and died of pneumonia.

Vocabulary

- **химию**: chemistry (accusative)
- **формулы**: formulas
- **даже**: even
- **если нет**: if not
- **таблицу Менделеева**: Mendeleev's table
- **изобрёл**: invented
- **учёный**: scientist
- **по фамилии**: by surname
- **узнать**: learn
- **читайте дальше**: read further (imperative)
- **полное**: full
- **Дмитрий Иванович**: Dmitry Ivanovich
- **отчество**: patronymic
- **значит**: means
- **отца**: father (genitive)
- **родился**: was born
- **в середине**: in the middle of
- **девятнадцатого века**: the nineteenth century
- **директором гимназии**: a gymnasium director
- **домохозяйкой**: housewife (ablative)
- **только представьте**: just imagine (imperative)
- **семнадцать детей**: seventeen children
- **великий**: great
- **химик**: chemist
- **последним**: last
- **умер**: died
- **маленьким мальчиком**: little boy (dative)
- **вырастила**: raised
- **одна**: alone
- **не только**: not only
- **кстати**: by the way
- **десять процентов**: ten percent
- **о сельском хозяйстве**: about agriculture
- **промышленности**: industry (genitive)
- **конструировал**: constructed
- **корабли**: ships
- **воздушные шары**: air balloons
- **а что насчёт**: and what about
- **личной жизни**: personal life

- **был женат**: was married
- **дважды**: twice
- **на восемь лет его старше**: eight years older than he
- **трое детей**: three kids
- **сорок два**: fourty two
- **влюбился в**: fell in love with
- **женщину**: woman (accusative)
- **всего шестнадцать**: only sixteen
- **родила**: gave birth to
- **четырёх**: four
- **удивительно**: amazing
- **ни одного потомка**: not a single descendant
- **несколько мифов**: a few myths
- **говорят**: they say
- **увидел**: saw
- **знаменитую**: famous
- **во сне**: in a dream
- **неправда**: not true
- **думал**: thought
- **двадцать лет**: twenty years
- **однажды**: one day
- **рассказали**: told
- **расстроился**: got upset
- **огромный труд**: tremendous work
- **изобрёл водку**: invented vodka
- **снова**: again
- **ложь**: lies
- **было сделано**: was done
- **до него**: before him
- **обожал**: loved, adored
- **классическую музыку**: classic music (accusative)
- **особенно**: especially
- **также**: also
- **делать что-нибудь**: do something
- **своими руками**: with his own hands
- **чемоданы**: suitcases
- **в старости**: in the old age
- **полностью слепым**: completely blind
- **продолжал**: continued
- **такие вещи**: such things
- **играл в шахматы**: played chess
- **в баню**: to banya
- **русскую сауну**: Russian sauna
- **чай**: tea
- **по рецепту**: according to recipe

- **толерантным человеком**: tolerant person (dative)
- **читал лекции**: gave lectures
- **удивительно**: surprising
- **для нашего времени**: for our time
- **не могли**: couldn't
- **высшее образование**: higher education
- **ненавидел**: hated
- **расизм**: racism
- **свободу**: freedom
- **Нобелевская премия**: Nobel prize
- **номинаций**: nominations (genitive)
- **конфликт**: conflict
- **с братьями**: with brothers
- **и наконец**: at last
- **парадокс**: paradox
- **не признавал**: didn't admit
- **медицину**: medicine (accusative)
- **не обращался к врачам**: didn't turn to doctors
- **отличное**: excellent
- **здоровье**: health
- **прожил**: lived
- **семьдесят два года**: seventy two years
- **причина**: reason
- **воспаление лёгких**: pneumonia

Questions about the story

1. Менделеев вырос без матери. Правда или ложь?
   Mendeleev grew up without a mother. True or false?

   a. Правда.
      True.

   b. Ложь.
      False.

2. Сколько жён было у Менделеева?
   How many wives did Mendeleev have?

   a. 2.
   b. 3.
   c. 4.
   d. 1.

3. Что из этого — миф?
   Which of these is a myth?

   a. Менделеев изобрёл таблицу элементов.
      Mendeleev invented the table of elements.

   b. Менделеев изобрёл водку.
      Mendeleev invented vodka.

   c. Менделеев конструировал корабли.
      Mendeleev constructed ships.

   d. Менделеев любил играть в шахматы.
      Mendeleev liked to play chess.

4. Менделеев ненавидел...
   Mendeleev hated...

   a. Женщин.
      Women.

b. Чай.
   Tea.

c. Высшее образование.
   Higher education.

d. Расизм.
   Racism.

5. **Менделеев умер из-за...**
   Mendeleev died because of...

   a. Медицины.
      Medicine.

   b. Химии.
      Chemistry.

   c. Воспаления лёгких.
      Pneumonia.

   d. Конфликта с братьями Нобелями.
      A conflict with Nobel brothers.

Answers

1. B
2. A
3. B
4. D
5. C

CHAPTER VI

Ты счастлива? — Are You Happy?

Эта **история** о моей **подруге Кате. Катя очень милая девушка.** Она **хорошо выглядит.** Она **занимается спортом** и **ведёт здоровый образ жизни. Катя всё делает** правильно. Не **ест после шести, бегает по утрам,** не **пьёт** кофе, не ест **сладкое,** ходит в **спортзал.**

Моя подруга **много работает.** Она не **замужем.** Она **редко** ходит в **кино** или **театр. Предпочитает** спорт.

Также Катя **экономная.** Она не **тратит** деньги **на развлечения.** Моя подруга **часто** покупает **косметику** и **одежду.** Но она **всегда ждёт скидок.** Ей **нравится** такая жизнь. Это её **решение.**

Но есть **одна проблема.** Катя **уверена,** что **все должны** жить **так.** Она **лучшая, самая красивая,** самая **успешная.**

Однажды мы **гуляли по парку.**

— Катя, ты **счастлива**? — спросила я.

— Счастлива? — **удивилась** она.

— Ты **никогда об этом не думала?**

— Мне нравится моя жизнь. У меня есть работа, деньги, я занимаюсь спортом...

— Нет, Катя. Ты не **ответила** на мой вопрос. Ты счастлива? Да или нет?

— Я не **знаю,** Маша. Это **сложный** вопрос. **А ты**?

— Да, — сказала я **уверенно**.

Я **заметила**, что Катя была **грустной**. Я **хотела** ей **помочь**. У меня был **план**.

— Ты **торопишься**? — спросила я.
— **Немного**. Ждёт работа с **документами**.
— Но **завтра выходной**.
— Да, но завтра я иду в спортзал.
— На **весь день**?
— Нет, **конечно** нет.
— **Тогда** у меня есть **идея**. **Сегодня** ты **отдыхаешь**. Никаких офисов, документов, — спортзалов и экономии. Ты должна меня **слушать**. **Согласна**?
— **Даже** не знаю.
— Не смотри на **часы**. **Времени** много.
— **Хорошо**.

Мы пошли в **кафе**. Я **заказала** пиццу и **шоколадное мороженое**. Катя знала: это **калорийно**. Но мы **договорились**. Она съела всё очень **быстро**.

— **Вкусно**? — спросила я.
— **Честно**? Очень!

Затем мы пошли в **магазин** одежды. Кате понравилось **красное платье**. Это был её **любимый цвет**.

— **Очень дорогое**, — сказала она.
— Катя, **зачем** ты работаешь? Зачем тебе деньги? Платье очень красивое.
— Может быть, подождать **сезона** скидок? Нет, я куплю его. Мне оно нравится. **Извини**, Маша. Ты **права**. Деньги — это не так **важно**.

Катя **заплатила** и **улыбнулась**. Она была **рада покупке**. Мы **вышли** из магазина.

— Кофе? — спросила Катя.

— Уже **семь** часов, подруга. Ты уверена?

— Да. У меня хорошее **настроение**. **Погода прекрасная**. Я даже не хочу **спать**.

Мы пришли в кафе. Я пошла в **уборную**. Катя хотела заказать кофе и **десерт**. Я вернулась. Катя была не **одна**. Она говорила с **мужчиной**. Он был **высокого роста**, с **тёмными волосами**. Очень красивый. Я **решила уйти**.

Я **позвонила** Кате утром. Она была **сонной**.

— **Десять** часов, **пора вставать**, подруга.

— Да, **потому что** у меня **свидание**.

— **Отлично! Рада за тебя**!

— **Спасибо** тебе, Маша. Я знаю **ответ** на вопрос.

— Какой?

— Да, я счастлива!

Сейчас Катя ведёт здоровый образ жизни. Ходит в кино и кафе с **мужем**. Любит свою работу. Она счастлива.

Краткое содержание истории

Это история о моей подруге Кате. Она ведёт здоровый образ жизни, много работает и экономит. Она уверена, что все должны жить так. Мы говорили о счастье. Она не знает, счастлива она или нет. Она была грустной, и я хотела ей помочь. Мы договорились, что сегодня она отдыхает без экономии. Мы пошли в кафе, съели пиццу и мороженое. Она купила дорогое красное платье и встретила мужчину в кафе. У неё было свидание. Сейчас она замужем. Она ведёт здоровый образ жизни. Она счастлива.

Summary of the story

This is a story about my friend Kate. She leads a healthy lifestyle, works a lot and is thrifty. She's sure — everyone must live this way. We spoke about happiness. She doesn't know if she's happy or not. She was sad, and I wanted to help her. We agreed — she's having a rest without trying to save money today. We went to a cafe, had a pizza and an ice-cream. She bought an expensive red dress and met a man in a cafe. She had a date. She's married now. She leads a healthy lifestyle. She's happy.

Vocabulary

- **история**: story
- **подруге Кате**: friend Kate (female prepositional)
- **очень милая девушка**: very nice girl
- **хорошо выглядит**: looks good
- **занимается спортом**: goes in for sports
- **ведёт здоровый образ жизни**: leads a healthy lifestyle
- **всё делает правильно**: does everything right
- **ест после шести**: eats after six
- **бегает по утрам**: takes morning runs
- **пьёт**: drinks
- **сладкое**: sweet
- **спортзал**: gym
- **много работает**: works a lot
- **замужем**: married
- **редко**: seldom

- **кино**: cinema
- **театр**: theatre
- **предпочитает**: prefers
- **экономная**: thrifty
- **тратит на развлечения**: spends on entertainment
- **часто**: often
- **косметику**: cosmetics (accusative)
- **одежду**: clothes (accusative)
- **всегда**: always
- **ждёт скидок**: waiting for discounts
- **нравится**: likes
- **решение**: decision
- **но**: but
- **одна проблема**: one problem
- **уверена**: sure
- **все должны**: everyone must
- **так**: this way
- **лучшая**: best

- **самая красивая**: most beautiful
- **успешная**: successful
- **однажды**: one day
- **гуляли по парку**: walked in the park
- **счастлива**: happy
- **удивилась**: was surprised
- **никогда об этом не думала**: never thought about that
- **ответила**: answered
- **знаю**: know
- **Маша**: Masha
- **сложный**: difficult
- **а ты**: and you
- **уверенно**: confidently
- **заметила**: noticed
- **грустной**: sad
- **хотела**: wanted
- **помочь**: help
- **план**: plan
- **торопишься**: in a hurry
- **немного**: a bit
- **документами**: documents (ablative)
- **завтра выходной**: tomorrow's a day off
- **весь день**: all day
- **конечно**: of course
- **тогда**: then
- **идея**: idea
- **сегодня**: today
- **отдыхаешь**: have a rest
- **никаких**: no
- **слушать**: listen
- **согласна**: agree
- **даже**: even
- **часы**: watch
- **времени**: time (genitive)
- **хорошо**: ok
- **кафе**: cafe
- **заказала**: ordered
- **шоколадное мороженое**: chocolate ice-cream
- **калорийно**: calorie
- **договорились**: agreed
- **быстро**: quickly

- **вкусно**: delicious

- **честно**: honestly

- **затем**: then

- **магазин**: shop

- **красное платье**: red dress

- **любимый цвет**: favorite color

- **очень дорогое**: very expensive

- **зачем**: why

- **сезона**: season (genitive)

- **извини**: sorry

- **права**: right

- **важно**: important

- **заплатила**: paid

- **улыбнулась**: smiled

- **рада**: glad

- **покупке**: purchase (dative)

- **вышли**: came out

- **семь**: seven

- **настроение**: mood

- **погода прекрасная**: weather is wonderful

- **спать**: sleep

- **уборную**: restroom (accusative)

- **десерт**: dessert

- **одна**: alone

- **мужчиной**: man (ablative)

- **высокого роста**: tall

- **тёмными волосами**: dark hair (ablative)

- **решила**: decided

- **уйти**: leave

- **позвонила**: called

- **сонной**: sleepy

- **десять**: ten

- **пора вставать**: time to wake up

- **потому что**: because

- **свидание**: date

- **отлично**: great

- **рада за тебя**: happy for you

- **спасибо**: thanks

- **ответ**: answer

- **мужем**: husband (ablative)

Questions about the story

1. **Есть одна проблема. Катя ленивая. Правда или ложь?**
    There's one problem. Kate is lazy. True or false?

    a. Правда.
        True.

    b. Ложь.
        False.

2. **Катя тратит деньги только на развлечения. Правда или ложь?**
    Kate spends money on entertainment only. True or false?

    a. Правда.
        True.

    b. Ложь.
        False.

3. **Какое мороженое ели Катя с Машей?**
    Which ice-cream did Kate and Masha eat?

    a. Шоколадное.
        Chocolate.

    b. Банановое.
        Banana.

    c. Яблочное.
        Apple.

    d. Ванильное.
        Vanilla.

4. **В магазине Катя купила...**
   At the shop Kate bought...

   a. Сумку.
      A bag.

   b. Пальто.
      A coat.

   c. Платье.
      A dress.

   d. Юбку.
      A skirt.

5. **Сейчас Катя ходит в кино и кафе с...**
   Now Kate goes to the cinema and cafe with...

   a. Машей.
      Masha.

   b. Папой.
      Father.

   c. Мамой.
      Mother.

   d. Мужем.
      Husband.

Answers

1. B
2. B
3. A
4. C
5. D

CHAPTER VII

Всё к лучшему —
It's All for the Best

Говорят, «**всё к лучшему**». Я **не верил** в эти **слова**.

Я собирался **лететь** в Москву на **собеседование. Работа мечты**! Я был очень **взволнован**. Вечером я завёл **будильник**, упаковал **чемодан** и **заранее вызвал** такси. Я хотел **проснуться в шесть утра**.

Я лёг **в постель**. Но у меня было много **мыслей**. Я не мог **уснуть**...

Меня **разбудил** телефон.

— Алло! Это такси. Я **жду** вас уже **полчаса**.

Я посмотрел **на часы. Половина седьмого**! Я быстро **оделся**, **схватил** чемодан и **побежал**.

«**Успокойся**, Сергей», — говорил я **сам себе**. — «Это не **конец света**».

Таксист понимал, что я **тороплюсь**. Он **ехал быстро**. Мне казалось, что **светофор** всё время был **красным**. Всё **против меня**!

Недалеко от аэропорта мы **застряли в пробке**. Я **просто** не мог ждать! Я **заплатил** таксисту и побежал.

Погода была **дождливой**, я **промок**, а мой **костюм** и **туфли** были все **в грязи**.

«**Не важно**», — думал я. — «Я куплю **новую одежду** в Москве. Сейчас моя **цель** — аэропорт».

Я добежал до **стойки регистрации**. Я **достал из** чемодана свой **паспорт** и **передал** его девушке. Мне не нужно было **показывать билет**: я купил **электронный**.

— **Извините**, но Вашего билета нет **в списке**, — сказала девушка.

Некоторое время я просто смотрел на неё. Мне хотелось **закричать**, но я **спросил**:

— **Вы уверены**? У меня **редкая фамилия**. Проверьте **ещё раз**, пожалуйста.

Девушка **согласилась**.

— Ах, да! — **воскликнула** девушка. Я подумал, что **всё будет хорошо**.

— Я **нашла** Ваш билет, но он **на завтра**.

Я не мог поверить своим **ушам**! Я **не получу** работу своей мечты, **потому что заказал** билет на **неверное число**!

Я извинился, забрал свой паспорт. Я **набрал номер** офиса и **объяснил** им ситуацию. Я **надеялся**, что они **пригласят** меня на новое собеседование. Но они не пригласили. Они **пожелали мне удачи**.

Я не мог **простить** себя за свою **ошибку**.

Мне не хотелось ехать домой. Мне не хотелось звонить **родителям** или своей **девушке**. Они скажут, что будут **другие возможности** и другие собеседования.

Я вышел из аэропорта, **поймал** такси и поехал в свой **любимый бар**. Я заказал коктейль и просто смотрел на **экран телевизора**... И **вдруг** я услышал **что-то о самолёте** в Москву. Я попросил бармена **сделать громче**.

Это был мой **рейс**. Рейс, на который я **опоздал**. Самолёт **разбился вскоре** после взлёта. **Трудно описать** мои эмоции! **Удивление, страх, радость** и... **Стыд**. Работа? Карьера? Я мог **умереть**!

Всю дорогу домой я звонил **родственникам** и друзьям. Они **знали** о моих планах и думали, что я **мёртв**. Моя ошибка **спасла** мне **жизнь**!

В тот день я **понял**, что всё к лучшему! И у меня два **дня рождения**!

Краткое содержание истории

Сергея пригласили в Москву на собеседование. Он всегда мечтал о такой работе. Он заказал электронный билет на самолёт. Сергей проспал, но ему удалось попасть в аэропорт вовремя. Но оказалось, что он заказал билет на другой день. Он очень расстроился. Сергей поехал в бар. В новостях он услышал, что самолёт, на который он опоздал, разбился вскоре после взлёта. Сергей понял, что его ошибка спасла ему жизнь.

Summary of the story

Sergey was invited to a job interview in Moscow. He had always dreamed of such a job. He ordered an electronic ticket to the plane. Sergey overslept, but he managed to get to the airport on time. But it turned out that he'd ordered a ticket for a different day. He was very upset. Sergey went to a bar. On the news he heard that the plane he had missed had crashed soon after the take-off. Sergey understood that his mistake had saved his life.

Vocabulary

- **всё к лучшему**: it's all for the best
- **не верил**: didn't believe
- **слова**: words
- **лететь**: fly
- **собеседование**: job interview
- **работа мечты**: dream job
- **взволнован**: excited
- **будильник**: alarm clock
- **чемодан**: suitcase
- **заранее**: beforehand
- **вызвал**: called
- **проснуться**: wake up
- **в шесть утра**: at six o'clock in the morning
- **в постель**: to bed
- **мыслей**: thoughts (plural genitive)
- **уснуть**: fall asleep
- **удалось**: managed (impersonal)
- **становилось**: was getting
- **разбудил**: woke up (transitive)
- **жду**: have been waiting
- **полчаса**: half an hour
- **на часы**: at the watch
- **половина седьмого**: half past six
- **оделся**: dressed (reflexive)
- **схватил**: grabbed
- **побежал**: ran
- **успокойся**: calm down (imperative)
- **сам себе**: to myself
- **конец света**: the end of the world
- **таксист**: taxi driver
- **тороплюсь**: I'm in a hurry
- **ехал быстро**: was driving fast
- **мне казалось**: it seemed to me
- **светофор**: traffic lights
- **красным**: red
- **против меня**: against me
- **недалеко от**: not far from
- **просто**: just
- **застряли в пробке**: got stuck in a traffic jam
- **заплатил**: paid
- **дождливой**: rainy
- **промок**: got wet
- **костюм**: suit
- **туфли**: shoes
- **в грязи**: in mud

- **не важно**: doesn't matter
- **новую одежду**: new clothes
- **цель**: goal
- **стойки регистрации**: check-in counter (genitive)
- **достал из**: took out of
- **паспорт**: passport
- **передал**: passed
- **показывать билет**: show the ticket
- **электронный**: electronic
- **извините**: sorry
- **в списке**: on the list
- **некоторое время**: for some time
- **закричать:**: start screaming
- **спросил**: asked
- **вы уверены**: are you sure
- **редкая фамилия**: rare surname
- **ещё раз**: one more time
- **согласилась**: agreed
- **воскликнула**: exclaimed
- **всё будет хорошо**: everything will be fine
- **нашла**: found
- **на завтра**: for tomorrow
- **ушам**: ears (plural dative)
- **не получу**: won't get

- **потому что**: because
- **заказал**: ordered
- **неверное число**: wrong date
- **набрал номер**: dialed the number
- **объяснил**: explained
- **надеялся**: hoped
- **пригласят**: will invite
- **пожелали мне удачи**: wished me good luck
- **простить**: forgive
- **ошибку**: mistake (accusative)
- **родителям**: parents (dative)
- **девушке**: girlfriend (dative)
- **другие возможности**: other opportunities
- **поймал**: caught
- **любимый бар**: favorite bar
- **экран телевизора**: TV screen
- **вдруг**: suddenly
- **что-то**: something
- **о самолёте в**: about the plane to
- **сделать громче**: turn up
- **рейс**: flight

- **опоздал**: missed
- **разбился**: crashed
- **вскоре**: soon
- **взлёта**: take-off (noun genitive)
- **трудно**: hard
- **описать**: describe
- **в тот момент**: at that moment
- **удивление**: surprise
- **страх**: fear
- **радость**: joy
- **стыд**: shame
- **умереть**: die
- **всю дорогу**: all the way
- **родственникам**: relatives (dative)
- **знали**: knew
- **мёртв**: dead
- **спасла**: saved
- **жизнь**: life
- **понял**: understood
- **дня рождения**: birthdays (genitive)

Questions about the story

1. **Зачем Сергей собирался лететь в Москву?**
   What was Sergey going to fly to Moscow for?

   a. На экскурсию.
      On an excursion.

   b. На собеседование.
      For a job interview.

   c. На свадьбу.
      To a wedding.

   d. За покупками.
      To go shopping.

2. **Во сколько Сергей проснулся?**
   At what time did Sergey wake up?

   a. 06:00.
   b. 07:00.
   c. 07:30.
   d. 06:30.

3. **Почему Сергей вышел из такси и бежал до аэропорта?**
   Why did Sergey get out of the taxi and ran to the airport?

   a. Они застряли в пробке.
      They were stuck in a traffic jam.

   b. Таксист ехал слишком медленно.
      The taxi driver was driving too slowly.

   c. Светофор сломался.
      The traffic lights were broken.

   d. Вокруг было слишком много пешеходов.
      There were too many pedestrians around.

4. Почему Сергей не показал девушке билет?
   Why didn't Sergey show the ticket to the girl?

   a. Он забыл его дома.
      He left it at home.

   b. Он потерял его.
      He lost it.

   c. Он заказал электронный билет.
      He ordered an electronic ticket.

   d. Кто-то украл его билет.
      Someone has stolen his ticket.

5. В конце Сергей был рад, что опоздал на самолёт. Правда или ложь?
   Finally, Sergey was happy he'd missed the flight. True or false?

   a. Правда.
   b. True.
   c. Ложь.
   d. False.

Answers

1. B
2. D
3. A
4. C
5. C

CHAPTER VIII

Настоящий мужчина — A Real Man

Меня зовут Олег. Я **много работаю**. После **тяжёлой недели всем** нужно **отдохнуть**. **Почти** каждые **выходные** я **провожу** в компании своих **друзей**. Мои друзья **шумные** и **весёлые парни**. Они **любят ходить** в **бары**, **пить пиво** или **крепкие напитки**, смотреть **футбольные матчи**, **играть** в **хоккей** и **говорить** о **красивых женщинах**.

Читатель, я **хочу поделиться** с тобой **секретом**. Я **терпеть не могу** выходные с парнями. В барах шумно, от крепких напитков **ужасно болит голова**, футбол для меня — **бесполезный спорт**. **Что дальше**? Хоккей? Не люблю **агрессивный** спорт. **Разговоры** о красивых женщинах меня не **интересуют**. **Самая красивая** женщина **на свете** — моя **жена**.

Кстати, о моей жене. Полина **ничего** об этом не **знала**. Я **уходил** к друзьям, а она меня **провожала**.

— Что будешь **делать вечером**? — **спросил** я.
— **Ещё** не **решила**. Может быть, **приму ванну** или **посмотрю** фильм. **Приготовлю** попкорн или **поем чипсов**. Оля **подарила** мне **новую маску** для лица. **Расслаблюсь немного**,
— ответила Полина.
— **Салон красоты** и **удовольствия**?
— **Что-то вроде**.

— Тогда **хорошего вечера, милая**.
— Спасибо, **тебе тоже, дорогой**.

Я **выходил** из **дома** и **понимал**: я хочу **вернуться**. Я **даже завидовал** Полине. **Никаких** шумных компаний и пива, **криков "гол"** и **глупых** разговоров. Она проводила время с удовольствием. Мне было **стыдно** сказать ей о своих **чувствах**. Я **стеснялся**. Я **мужчина. Брутальный, сильный** и **независимый**. Никаких масок для лица, **мелодрам** и **розочек**.

Но однажды друзья **отменили встречу**. Все были **заняты** на работе. Я мог **остаться** дома **вместе** с Полиной.

— **Давай** проведём этот вечер **спокойно**, — **предложил** я.
— Я **всегда** провожу выходные спокойно, — ответила Полина.
— **Отлично**. Что будем делать?

Мы делали **всё**. Полина предложила посмотреть «**Титаник**». Мы пили не пиво, не крепкие напитки. Жена сделала **вкусный травяной чай**, приготовила **наггетсы**. Мы **обсудили** фильм. Это было **прекрасно**.

— Я буду делать маску для лица. А ты? — **улыбнулась** Полина.
— Я **тоже** буду, — ответил я.
— Отлично. **Приготовься** к **увлажнению**, мужчина.

Мне было весело. Я принял ванну. Мы говорили о **жизни**. Я был **абсолютно счастлив**. Я рассказал Полине всё. Она не **удивилась**. Она хорошо меня знала и всегда **понимала**. В тот вечер я понял — это **настоящий** я. И это хорошо.

После этого я **иногда пропускал** встречи с друзьями. Мы с женой ходим в **бассейн, катаемся на велосипедах, выращиваем овощи** и **фрукты**. В баре я **заказываю апельсиновый сок** и мои друзья всё знают. **Некоторые** из них тоже **попробовали** провести время с жёнами. Они сказали мне спасибо. Парни **редко**

обсуждают женщин. Они поняли, что проводить время с жёнами интересно.

Главное в жизни — **быть собой.**

Краткое содержание истории

Меня зовут Олег. Я провожу выходные с друзьями. Мы ходим в бары, пьём крепкие напитки, смотрим футбольные матчи. Мне это не нравится. Я завидую жене: она остаётся дома и расслабляется. Однажды я остался с ней. Мы хорошо провели время. Я принял ванну и посмотрел «Титаник». Я всё рассказал жене. Она меня поняла. Теперь я заказываю в баре апельсиновый сок и чаще провожу выходные с женой. Мои друзья тоже проводят время с жёнами. Главное — быть собой.

Summary of the story

My name's Oleg. I spend weekends with friends. We go to the bars, drink hard spirits, watch football matches. I don't like it. I envy my wife: she stays at home and relaxes. One day I stayed with her. We had a good time. I had a bath and watched "Titanic". I told my wife everything. She understood me. Now I order orange juice at the bar and spend weekends with my wife more often. My friends also spend time with their wives. The main thing is to be yourself.

Vocabulary

- **настоящий мужчина**: real man
- **много**: a lot
- **работаю**: work
- **тяжёлой**: hard
- **недели**: week (genitive)
- **всем**: everyone (dative)
- **отдохнуть**: rest
- **почти**: almost
- **выходные**: weekends
- **провожу**: spend
- **друзей**: friends (genitive)
- **шумные**: noisy
- **весёлые**: funny
- **парни**: guys
- **любят**: love
- **ходить**: go
- **бары**: bars
- **пить**: drink
- **пиво**: beer
- **крепкие напитки**: hard spirits
- **футбольные матчи**: football matches
- **играть**: play
- **хоккей**: hockey
- **говорить**: speak
- **красивых**: beautiful
- **женщинах**: women (prepositional)
- **читатель**: reader
- **хочу**: want
- **поделиться**: share
- **секретом**: secret (ablative)
- **терпеть не могу**: can't stand
- **ужасно болит голова**: have a terrible headache
- **бесполезный**: useless
- **спорт**: sport
- **что дальше**: what's next
- **агрессивный**: aggressive
- **разговоры**: talks
- **интересуют**: get interested
- **самая красивая**: most beautiful
- **на свете**: in the world
- **жена**: wife
- **кстати**: by the way
- **ничего**: nothing
- **знала**: knew
- **уходил**: went away
- **провожала**: saw off
- **делать**: do
- **вечером**: in the evening
- **спросил**: asked

- **ещё**: yet
- **решила**: decided
- **приму ванну**: will have bath
- **посмотрю фильм**: will watch film
- **приготовлю**: will cook
- **попкорн**: popcorn
- **поем**: will eat
- **чипсов**: chips (genitive)
- **подарила**: gave (about a present)
- **новую**: new
- **маску**: mask (accusative)
- **лица**: face (genitive)
- **расслаблюсь**: will relax
- **немного**: a bit
- **салон красоты**: beauty salon
- **удовольствия**: pleasure (genitive)
- **что-то вроде**: kind of
- **хорошего вечера**: have a good evening
- **милая**: honey
- **тебе тоже**: same to you
- **дорогой**: darling
- **выходил**: went out
- **дома**: house (genitive)
- **понимал**: understood
- **вернуться**: come back
- **даже**: even
- **завидовал**: envied
- **никаких криков**: no screams
- **гол**: goal
- **глупых**: silly
- **стыдно**: ashamed
- **чувствах**: feelings (prepositional plural)
- **стеснялся**: was embarrassed
- **мужчина**: man
- **брутальный**: brutal
- **сильный**: strong
- **независимый**: independent
- **мелодрам**: melodrama (genitive plural)
- **розочек**: little roses (genitive plural)
- **но**: but
- **однажды**: one day
- **отменили**: canceled
- **встречу**: meeting (accusative)
- **заняты**: busy
- **остаться**: stay
- **вместе**: together
- **давай**: let's
- **спокойно**: quietly
- **предложил**: suggested

- **всегда**: always
- **отлично**: great
- **всё**: everything
- **титаник**: titanic
- **вкусный**: delicious
- **травяной чай**: herbal tea
- **наггетсы**: nuggets
- **обсудили**: discussed
- **прекрасно**: wonderful
- **улыбнулась**: smiled
- **тоже**: too
- **приготовься**: get ready (imperative)
- **увлажнению**: moisturizing (dative)
- **жизни**: life (prepositional)
- **абсолютно**: absolutely
- **счастлив**: happy
- **удивилась**: was surprised

- **понимала**: understood
- **настоящий**: real
- **после**: after
- **иногда**: sometimes
- **пропускал**: skipped
- **бассейн**: swimming pool
- **катаемся на велосипедах**: ride bikes
- **выращиваем**: grow
- **овощи**: vegetables
- **фрукты**: fruits
- **заказываю**: order
- **апельсиновый сок**: orange juice
- **некоторые**: some
- **попробовали**: tried
- **редко**: rarely
- **главное**: main thing
- **быть собой**: be yourself

Questions about the story

1. **Что не нравится Олегу?**
   What doesn't Oleg like?

   a. Проводить время с женой.
      Spending time with a wife.

   b. Пить крепкие напитки.
      Drinking hard spirits.

   c. Быть дома на выходных.
      Staying at home on weekends.

   d. Пить апельсиновый сок.
      Drinking orange juice.

2. **Олег ничего не стесняется. Правда или ложь?**
   Oleg isn't ashamed of anything. True or false?

   a. Правда.
      True.

   b. Ложь.
      False.

3. **Как проводит свободное время Полина?**
   How does Polina spend her free time?

   a. Ходит по магазинам.
      Goes shopping.

   b. Встречается с подругами.
      Meets friends.

   c. Расслабляется дома.
      Relaxes at home.

   d. Устраивает вечеринки.
      Throws parties.

4. Олег поделился своим секретом с женой. Она его
    поняла. Правда или ложь?
    **Oleg shared his secret with his wife. She understood him.
    True or false?**

    a. Правда.
        True.

    b. Ложь.
        False.

5. **Как изменились друзья Олега?**
    How did Oleg's friends change?

    a. Они перестали видеться с Олегом.
        The stopped meeting Oleg.

    b. Они не изменились.
        They didn't change.

    c. Они не пьют крепкие напитки.
        They don't drink hard spirits.

    d. Они проводят больше времени с жёнами.
        They spend more time with wives.

Answers

1. B
2. B
3. C
4. A
5. D

CHAPTER IX

Богатый человек — A Rich Man

Максим — **богатый** человек. Он живёт **в роскошном особняке**. Он не покупает **одежду** и **обувь в магазинах**. У него есть **личный портной**. А ещё личная **охрана**, личный **повар**, личный **тренер**, личный **водитель** и личный **вертолёт**.

Максим ест **в дорогих ресторанах** и ездит на дорогих машинах. У него нет **жены**. Нет детей. Его **бизнес** — это его **семья**, его **жизнь**.

Однажды Максим собирался **на деловую встречу** в **другой** город. Он **хотел** лететь на своём вертолёте. Это **быстро** и **удобно**. Максим **проверил прогноз погоды**. **Туман**, дождь и **сильный ветер**. **Авиакомпании отменили** все рейсы.

— О, нет! **Придётся** ехать на машине! — сказал Максим **вслух**.

Он позвонил своему **водителю** и **предупредил** его.

— **Сколько займёт дорога**? — спросил его Максим.
— С **такой** погодой... Часов **семь-восемь**, — ответил водитель.
— Если **без остановок**.
— Какие остановки?! — спросил Максим **с раздражением**. — **Перекусить в придорожном кафе**? Нет, спасибо!

Прогноз погоды не **соврал**. Погода была **ужасной**. Они ехали **медленно**. Максим **нервничал**. Это была очень **важная** встреча. **Через несколько часов** они остановились.

— Нужно **подождать**, — **объяснил** водитель, — Я **не вижу дороги**.

— **Ладно**.

— Я **пока** перекушу.

— **Давай**. Перекусывай.

— Моя жена **приготовила мясной пирог**. Не хотите **кусочек**?

Максим посмотрел на него **с презрением**.

— Я не ем такую **еду**. Ты знаешь это. Я **поужинаю** в ресторане.

— Ладно. Я **просто спросил**, — сказал водитель и **с удовольствием** съел пирог.

Максим **успел** на свою встречу. **После** встречи он поужинал в ресторане. Это был **самый дорогой** ресторан в городе. **Как обычно**. Утром они поехали **обратно** домой. Погода **не стала лучше**. Они ехали медленно. Через несколько часов машина остановилась.

— **Почему** мы остановились? — спросил Максим.

— **Что-то не так** с машиной, — ответил водитель. — Я выйду **посмотрю**.

Он скоро вернулся.

— Серьёзные **проблемы с мотором**. Придётся **вызывать эвакуатор**.

— **Ты с ума сошёл**?! — **закричал** Максим, — Я возвращаюсь домой на эвакуаторе! Это будет **во всех газетах**! Все будут **смеяться** надо мной! Ты можешь **починить** мотор?

— Да, но мне нужны **детали**.

Максим вызвал **такси** и его водитель **уехал в город** купить детали. **Прошёл час**, два, три... Водитель не возвращался. Что могло **случиться**? Наконец Максим увидел такси.

— **Где ты был**? — спросил он **со злостью**.

— **Извините, долго искал** детали. Сейчас, **час-два** и поедем.

— Час-два?! Я **устал** и **хочу есть**!

— Я сделал **бутерброды**. Хотите?

— Я **подожду**! Я не ем **такое**.

Водитель починил машину. Погода стала **хуже**. Они ехали **ещё медленнее**.

— Когда мы будем дома? — спросил Максим. — Я **умираю от голода**.

— Через четыре часа. **Если повезёт**, — ответил водитель. — **Скоро** будет **небольшое** кафе. Хорошее **место**. Называется «**Еда, как дома**». **Вкусная** еда.

Максим **засомневался**. Может, **попробовать**? Но это придорожное кафе!

— Ладно, — **согласился** он. — Ещё четыре часа. Это **слишком много**...

Это был не ресторан, но **уютно** и **тепло**.

Перед Максимом стояла **тарелка** — **картофельное пюре** и **тушёная курица**. Для Максима блюдо выглядело **бледным** и **непривлекательным**. Он **попробовал** и **ничего** не сказал...

Через несколько дней водитель Максима **встретил** его **горничную**.

— Я думаю, — сказала она, — мы скоро **потеряем работу**.

— Почему? — **удивился** водитель.

— У **хозяина мало денег**, — ответила горничная.

— Почему ты так думаешь?

— **Смотри**, я **заметила** это **в мусорном ведре**. Это **не первый раз**. — Она **показала** водителю **бумажный пакет**. На пакете **было написано** «Еда, как дома».

— **Не волнуйся**, — ответил водитель. — **Дело не в этом**.

И он рассказал ей **историю** с придорожным кафе.

Краткое содержание истории

Максим очень богатый человек. У него роскошный дом. У него есть личный портной и личный вертолёт. Он ест только в дорогих ресторанах.

Однажды Максим собирался на деловую встречу в другой город. Он хотел лететь на вертолёте. Но погода была слишком плохая. Он поехал на машине с водителем. После встречи Максим поужинал в ресторане. На следующий день они возвращались обратно. Машина сломалась. Водитель мог починить её, но ему нужны были детали. Водитель поехал в соседний город на такси. Максим ждал его три часа. Он устал. Он хотел есть. Водитель предложил ему поесть в придорожном кафе «Еда, как дома». Он согласился. Максим попробовал картофельное пюре и тушёную курицу.

Через несколько дней горничная Максима сказала водителю, что у хозяина мало денег. Она заметила в его мусорном ведре бумажные пакеты с надписью «Еда, как дома». Водитель рассказал ей историю с придорожным кафе.

Summary of the story

Maxim is a very rich man. He has a luxurious house. He has a personal tailor and a personal helicopter. He eats only in expensive restaurants.

One day Maxim was going to a business meeting in another city. He wanted to fly by helicopter. But the weather was too bad. He went by car with a driver. After the meeting, Maxim had supper in a restaurant. Next day they were coming back. The car broke down. The driver could fix it, but he needed the spare parts. The driver went to the neighboring town by taxi. Maxim had been waiting for

91

him for three hours. He was tired. He was hungry. The driver offered him to eat in a roadside cafe 'Food like at home'. He agreed. Maxim tried mashed potatoes and stewed chicken. He ate all.

In a few days, Maxim's housemaid told the driver that the master had little money. She noticed paper bags in his waste bin with the inscription 'Food like at home'. The driver told her the story about the roadside cafe.

Vocabulary

- **богатый**: rich
- **всегда**: always
- **в роскошном особняке**: in a luxurious mansion
- **одежду**: clothes (accusative)
- **обувь**: footwear (accusative)
- **в магазинах**: in shops
- **личный**: personal
- **портной**: tailor
- **охрана**: security
- **повар**: cook
- **тренер**: coach
- **водитель**: driver
- **вертолёт**: helicopter
- **в дорогих ресторанах**: in expensive restaurants
- **ездит**: drives
- **жены**: wife (genitive)
- **бизнес**: business
- **семья**: family
- **жизнь**: life
- **однажды**: onc day
- **на деловую встречу**: to a business meeting
- **другой**: another
- **хотел**: wanted
- **быстро**: quickly
- **удобно**: comfortably

- **проверил**: checked
- **прогноз погоды**: weather forecast
- **туман**: fog
- **сильный ветер**: strong wind
- **авиакомпании**: airline companies
- **отменили**: cancelled
- **придётся**: will have to
- **вслух**: aloud
- **водителю**: driver (dative)
- **предупредил**: warned
- **сколько займёт дорога**: how much will the road take
- **такой**: such
- **семь-восемь**: seven or eight
- **без остановок**: without stops
- **с раздражением**: with irritation
- **перекусить**: have a snack
- **в придорожном кафе**: in a roadside cafe
- **соврал**: lied
- **ужасной**: terrible
- **медленно**: slowly
- **нервничал**: was nervous

- **важная**: important
- **через несколько часов**: in a few hours
- **подождать**: wait
- **не вижу дороги**: don't see the road
- **объяснил**: explained
- **ладно**: ok
- **пока**: meanwhile
- **давай**: go ahead
- **приготовила**: cooked
- **мясной пирог**: meat pie
- **кусочек**: piece
- **с презрением**: with contempt
- **еду**: food (accusative)
- **поужинаю**: will have supper
- **просто спросил**: just asked
- **с удовольствием**: with pleasure
- **успел**: managed to come in time
- **после**: after
- **самый дорогой**: the most expensive
- **как обычно**: as usual
- **обратно**: back
- **не стала лучше**: didn't get better
- **почему**: why
- **что-то не так**: something is wrong
- **вернулся**: returned
- **посмотрю**: will take a look
- **проблемы**: problems
- **с мотором**: with the engine
- **вызывать**: call
- **эвакуатор**: tow truck
- **ты с ума сошёл**: have you gone mad
- **закричал**: shouted
- **во всех газетах**: in all the newspapers
- **смеяться**: laugh
- **починить**: fix
- **детали**: spare parts
- **такси**: taxi
- **уехал в город**: left for the city
- **купить**: buy
- **час**: hour
- **случиться**: happen
- **где ты был**: where have you been
- **со злостью**: with anger
- **извините**: excuse me
- **долго искал**: was looking for a long time
- **час-два**: hour or two
- **устал**: tired
- **хочу есть**: am hungry

- **бутерброды**: sandwiches
- **подожду**: will wait
- **такое**: such things
- **хуже**: worse
- **ещё медленнее**: still more slowly
- **умираю от голода**: am starving
- **если повезёт**: if we're lucky
- **скоро**: soon
- **небольшое**: small
- **место**: place
- **еда как дома**: food like at home
- **вкусная**: delicious
- **засомневался**: started to doubt
- **согласился**: agreed
- **слишком много**: too much
- **уютно**: cozy
- **тепло**: warm
- **перед**: in front
- **тарелка**: plate
- **картофельное пюре**: potato mash
- **тушёная курица**: stewed chicken
- **бледным**: pale

- **непривлекательным**: unattractive
- **попробовал**: tried
- **ничего**: nothing
- **встретил**: met
- **горничную**: housemaid (accusative)
- **потеряем работу**: will lose job
- **удивился**: surprised
- **хозяина**: master (genitive)
- **мало денег**: little money
- **смотри**: look (imperative)
- **заметила**: noticed
- **в мусорном ведре**: in the waste bin
- **не первый раз**: not the first time
- **показала**: showed
- **бумажный пакет**: paper bag
- **было написано**: was written
- **не волнуйся**: don't worry (imperative)
- **дело не в этом**: it's not about it
- **историю**: story (accusative)

Questions about the story

1. **У Максима есть семья. Правда или ложь?**
    Maxim has a family. True or false?

    a. Правда.
        True.

    b. Ложь.
        False.

2. **Почему Максим не полетел на вертолёте?**
    Why didn't Maxim fly by helicopter?

    a. Вертолёт сломался.
        The helicopter broke down.

    b. Он не любит летать на самолёте.
        He doesn't fly by plane.

    c. Погода была плохая.
        The weather was bad.

    d. Он выбрал авиакомпанию.
        He chose an airline company.

3. **Почему Максим не перекусил пирогом водителя?**
    Why didn't Maxim snack on the driver's pie?

    a. Он не ест такую еду.
        He doesn't eat such food.

    b. Он не знал, кто его приготовил.
        He didn't know who had cooked it.

    c. Он не хотел есть в машине.
        He didn't want to eat in the car.

    d. Он не хотел есть.
        He wasn't hungry.

4. **Максим вернулся домой на эвакуаторе. Правда или ложь?**
   Maxim returned home by a tow truck. True or false?

   a. Правда.
      True.

   b. Ложь.
      False.

5. **Максиму понравилась еда из придорожного кафе?**
   Did Maxim like the food from the roadside cafe?

   a. Нет, она была непривлекательная.
      No, it was unattractive.

   b. Да, и он сказал об этом своему водителю.
      Yes, and he told the driver about it.

   c. Да, и он сказал об этом горничной.
      Yes, and he told the housemaid about it.

   d. Да, он покупал её опять.
      Yes, he bought it again.

Answers

1. B
2. C
3. A
4. B
5. D

CHAPTER X

Достоевский — Dostoevsky

Фёдор Михайлович Достоевский — **знаменитый писатель**. Он **мечтал стать** писателем в **детстве**. С детства **любимым** писателем Достоевского был **Александр Сергеевич Пушкин**. Он **знал некоторые** его **стихотворения наизусть**. Достоевский **считал** детство **лучшим временем** своей **жизни**.

В **семье** Достоевских было **восемь детей**. Семья писателя была не **богата**, но **родители дали** детям **хорошее образование**. **К сожалению**, папу Фёдора Михайловича **убили**. **Мать** писателя **умерла** от **туберкулёза**. Ему было 16.

В 1849 году Достоевского **приговорили к смертной казни**. Он был **против правительства**. Но писателю **повезло**. Казнь **отменили**. **Однако** Фёдор Михайлович **провёл на каторге** 4 года. Он был **болен**. У писателя была **эпилепсия**.

Писатель был **дважды женат**. **Первый раз** он женился в 36 лет. **Супруги развелись через семь лет. Интересный факт: вторая жена** Достоевского **Анна** была **моложе** его на 25 лет. Со второй женой у писателя было **четыре** ребёнка.

Достоевский был **азартным человеком**. **Поэтому** Анна **вела** все его **финансовые дела**. Она **очень помогла** писателю. **Благодаря** ей он **бросил** азартные **игры**.

Фёдор Михайлович **отдал всю** свою жизнь **литературе**. Он **всегда что-то писал**. Писал он **чаще всего ночью**.

Самая знаменитая книга писателя — «Преступление и наказание». Этот **роман** дети **изучают** в **школе**. Достоевский был **религиозным** человеком. Это **отражено** в его книге.

Писатель стал знаменитым только **после смерти. Ницше** считал Достоевского **лучшим психологом. Зигмунд Фрейд** сравнивал Достоевского с **Шекспиром** и **называл «Братья Карамазовы» величайшим** романом **в мире**.

Фёдор Михайлович Достоевский за свою жизнь **побывал** в **Италии**, в **Австрии**, в **Англии**, в **Швейцарии**, в **Германии** и во **Франции**.

Умер Фёдор Михайлович в 1881 году. **Диагноз** — туберкулёз. После смерти писателя его жена **больше не вышла замуж**.

О писателе **было снято** много **фильмов**. Произведения Достоевского отражены в **балете**, **опере** и **театре**.

Краткое содержание истории

Фёдор Михайлович Достоевский — великий русский писатель. Его семья не была богата. Но родители дали детям хорошее образование. Достоевского приговорили к смертной казни. Позже её отменили. Писатель провёл четыре года на каторге. Он был дважды женат. У него было четверо детей. Он всю жизнь писал. О писателе снято много фильмов. Он умер от туберкулёза.

Summary of the story

Fyodor Michaylovich Dostoevsky is a great Russian writer. His family wasn't rich. But the parents gave their children good education. Dostoevsky was sentenced to death. The sentence was overturned. The writer spent four years at a forced labor camp. He was married twice. He had four children. He had been writing during his whole life. Lots of films are shot about the writer. He died of tuberculosis.

Vocabulary

- **Фёдор Михайлович Достоевский**: Fyodor Michaylovich Dostoevsky
- **знаменитый**: famous
- **писатель**: writer
- **мечтал стать**: dreamed to become
- **детстве**: childhood (prepositional)
- **любимым**: favorite
- **Александр Сергеевич Пушкин**: Alexander Sergeyevich Pushkin
- **знал**: knew
- **некоторые**: some
- **стихотворения**: poems
- **наизусть**: by heart
- **считал**: considered
- **лучшим временем**: best time (ablative)
- **жизни**: life (prepositional)
- **семье**: family (prepositional)
- **восемь детей**: eight children
- **богата**: rich (short form)
- **родители**: parents
- **дали**: gave
- **хорошее**: good
- **образование**: education
- **к сожалению**: unfortunately
- **папу**: father (accusative)
- **убили**: murdered
- **мать**: mother
- **умерла**: died
- **туберкулёза**: tuberculosis (genitive)
- **приговорили к смертной казни**: sentenced to death
- **против правительства**: against the government (genitive)
- **повезло**: was lucky
- **отменили**: canceled
- **однако**: however
- **провёл**: spent
- **на каторге**: at a forced labor camp
- **болен**: ill (short form)
- **эпилепсия**: epilepsy
- **дважды**: twice
- **женат**: married (only about a man)
- **первый раз**: first time
- **супруги**: spouse

- **развелись**: got divorced
- **через семь лет**: in seven years
- **интересный**: interesting
- **факт**: fact
- **вторая**: second
- **жена**: wife
- **Анна**: Ann
- **моложе**: yonger
- **четыре**: four
- **азартным человеком**: gambler (ablative)
- **поэтому**: that's why
- **вела финансовые дела**: dealt with finances
- **очень помогла**: helped a lot
- **благодаря**: thanks to
- **бросил**: gave up
- **игры**: games
- **отдал**: gave
- **всю**: whole
- **литературе**: literature (dative)
- **всегда**: always
- **что-то**: something
- **писал**: wrote
- **чаще всего**: most often
- **ночью**: at night
- **самая знаменитая**: the most famous
- **«Преступление и наказание»**: "Crime and Punishment"
- **роман**: novel
- **изучают**: study
- **школе**: school (prepositional)
- **религиозным**: religious
- **отражено**: reflected
- **после смерти**: after death
- **Ницше**: Nietzsche
- **лучшим психологом**: the best psychologist (ablative)
- **Зигмунд Фрейд**: Sigmund Freud
- **сравнивал**: compared
- **Шекспиром**: Shakesphere
- **называл**: called
- **«Братья Карамазовы»**: "The Karamazov Brothers"
- **величайшим**: the greatest
- **в мире**: in the world (prepositional)
- **побывал**: visited

- **Италии**: Italy
  (prepositional)
- **Австрии**: Austria
  (prepositional)
- **Англии**: England
  (prepositional)
- **Швейцарии**:
  Switzerland
  (prepositional)
- **Германии**: Germany
  (prepositional)
- **Франции**: France
  (prepositional)
- **диагноз**: diagnosis
- **больше не вышла
  замуж**: didn't get
  married anymore
- **было снято**: was shot
- **фильмов**: films
  (genitive)
- **балете**: ballet
  (prepositional)
- **опере**: opera
  (prepositional)
- **театре**: theatre
  (prepositional)

Questions about the story

1. **Кем мечтал стать Достоевский?**
   What did Dostoevsky dream to be?

   a. Инженером.
      An engineer.

   b. Путешественником.
      A traveler.

   c. Учителем литературы.
      A teacher of literature.

   d. Писателем.
      A writer.

2. **Достоевский провёл на каторге два года. Правда или ложь?**
   Dostoevsky spent two years at a forced labor camp. True or false?

   a. Правда.
      True.

   b. Ложь.
      False.

3. **Что помогла бросить Достоевскому жена Анна?**
   What did Dostoevsky's wife Ann help him to give up?

   a. Азартные игры.
      Gambling.

   b. Алкоголь.
      Alcohol.

   c. Наркотики.
      Drugs.

d. Курение.
Smoking.

4. **От чего умер писатель?**
What did the writer die of?

a. Сердечный приступ.
Heart attack.

b. Туберкулёз.
Tuberculosis.

c. Астма.
Asthma.

d. Его убили.
He was murdered.

5. **Достоевский был очень знаменитым до смерти. Правда или ложь?**
Dostoevsky was very famous before death. True or false?

a. Правда.
True.

b. Ложь.
False.

Answers

1. D
2. B
3. A
4. B
5. B

CHAPTER XI

Внешность бывает обманчива — Appearances Can Be Deceptive

У меня есть **коллега**. Его зовут Миша и он любит **путешествовать**. **В прошлом году** он летал в **США**. Посмотреть **Большой каньон**. Мы **с нетерпением ждали** его **возвращения**. Он **обещал** показать фотографии, рассказать **о стране и людях**.

Миша **вернулся**. Мы пошли **в бар после работы**. У Миши была **классная поездка**! Он **выглядел** очень счастливым **на фотках**. Он рассказывал о **достопримечательностях**, людях, культуре, **местной кухне**.

— Мне всё **очень понравилось**! Люди были очень **вежливыми** и **дружелюбными**. И у меня было **приключение**!

Он **поехал** к Большому каньону **на машине**. Он **взял на прокат** **внедорожник**. Миша **отказался** брать **навигатор**. Ему нравятся обычные **карты**. Мой коллега **наслаждался**. **Пустыня, кактусы**... Но **вскоре** ему **стало скучно**. Он **свернул с трассы** и поехал по пустыне. **Пыль, песок, жара**... «Я **почти ковбой**», — думал Миша.

Но вскоре ковбой **застрял** в песке. Миша **вышел из** машины. Он **оглянулся. Ужас**! Он **не видел дороги**! **Нигде**! Он посмотрел на мобильный — **нет сети. Что делать? Сидеть у** машины и **ждать помощи**? Но **откуда**? Миша взял **рюкзак**. Он положил в него **паспорт**, **пару бутылок** воды, **бумажник** и телефон. Солнце, жара, пыль, **страх**...

Он шёл **весь день**. Стало **темно** и **прохладно**. Миша сел на песок. Он **ужасно устал**. Он был **напуган**. **Ночь** была **очень холодной**. Утром Миша **дошёл** до **шоссе**. Он **надеялся**, что **кто-нибудь** остановится и **подберёт** его. Но машины **не останавливались**. Миша **пошёл пешком**. **Через пару часов** он дошёл до **заправки**. «Сейчас спрошу, **где я**, **вызову такси** и доеду до **отеля**». Он увидел **пожилую** женщину. Она **заправляла** свою машину. Он **спросил** её:

— **Простите, вы не подскажете**...

Но она **отвернулась** и быстро **села в машину**. Миша спрашивал **других людей** — **та же самая** реакция. **Почему?** Миша **зашёл в здание. Никакой** помощи!

Он **вышел на улицу**. **Что происходит?** Он сел у здания и **услышал голос**.

— Что ты **хочешь** спросить?

Миша **поднял глаза** и увидел **бездомного** мужчину. Он **выглядел** ужасно. И **пах так же**. Но он был **готов** помочь. Бездомный **объяснил** Мише, **где он находится** и **дал номер** такси.

— Почему **никто** не помог мне? — спросил Миша.
— Они **думали**, что ты **такой как я**, — ответил мужчина.
— Я? Как ты? — **удивился** Миша.
— Посмотри на своё **отражение**.

Ну конечно! Столько времени в пустыне! Миша был **грязным**, его одежда была **порвана**, и он **плохо** пах. Люди **решили, что** он бездомный.

— Я понял, что **внешность бывает обманчива**. Тот бездомный **оказался отличным парнем**. А **те** люди... Они выглядели хорошо. Они хорошо пахли. Но никто не хотел мне помочь. **К**

несчастью, такое может **случиться** в **любой** стране. И ещё **мне** интересно: как **бы** я **себя** повёл?

Краткое содержание истории

У рассказчика есть коллега. Его зовут Миша. Он любит путешествовать. В прошлом году он ездил в Большой каньон. По дороге в каньон он решил проехать по пустыне. Его машина застряла в песке. Дороги нигде не было видно. Он не мог позвонить, потому что не было сети. Он пошёл пешком. Миша ночевал в пустыне.

Утром он вышел к шоссе. Ни одна машина не остановилась и не подобрала его. Он дошёл до заправки. Миша хотел узнать, где находится. Никто на заправке не хотел слушать его. Миша не понимал, что происходит. Затем к нему подошёл бездомный мужчина. Мужчина сказал Мише, где он находится и дал ему номер такси. Миша понял, что внешность бывает обманчива. Люди, которые хорошо выглядели, не помогли ему. А бездомный помог.

Summary of the story

The narrator has a colleague. His name is Misha. He likes traveling. Last year he went to The Grand Canyon. On the way to the canyon, he decided to drive through the desert. His car got stuck in the sand. He couldn't see the road anywhere. He was unable to make a call as there was no coverage. He went on foot. Misha spent the night in the desert.

In the morning, he came to the highway. No car stopped to pick him up. He went to a filling station. Misha wanted to find out where he was. No one at the filling station wanted to listen to him. Misha couldn't understand what was going on. Then a homeless man came up to him. The man told Misha where he was and gave him a taxi number. Misha understood that appearances can be deceptive. The people who looked good didn't help him. But a homeless man did.

Vocabulary

- **внешность бывает обманчива**: appearances can be deceptive
- **коллега**: colleague
- **путешествовать**: travel
- **в прошлом году**: last year
- **США**: the USA
- **Большой каньон**: The Grand Canyon
- **с нетерпением ждали**: were looking forward to
- **возвращения**: return (genitive)
- **обещал**: promised
- **о стране и людях**: about the country and the people
- **вернулся**: returned
- **в бар**: to the bar
- **после работы**: after work
- **классная поездка**: cool trip
- **выглядел**: looked
- **на фотках**: in the pics (colloquial)
- **достопримечательностях**: sights (prepositional)
- **о местной кухне**: about the local cuisine
- **очень понравилось**: liked a lot
- **вежливыми**: polite
- **дружелюбными**: friendly
- **приключение**: adventure
- **поехал к**: went to
- **на машине**: by car
- **взял на прокат внедорожник**: rented an offroader
- **отказался**: refused
- **навигатор**: GPS navigator
- **карты**: maps
- **наслаждался**: was enjoying
- **пустыня**: desert
- **кактусы**: cacti
- **вскоре**: soon
- **стало скучно**: got bored
- **свернул с трассы**: pull off the road
- **пыль**: dust
- **песок**: sand
- **жара**: heat
- **почти**: almost
- **ковбой**: cowboy
- **застрял**: got stuck
- **вышел из**: got out of
- **оглянулся**: looked around

- **ужас**: horror
- **не видел дороги**: didn't see the road
- **нигде**: nowhere
- **нет сети**: no coverage
- **что делать**: what should I do
- **сидеть у**: sit by
- **ждать помощи**: wait for help
- **откуда**: where from
- **рюкзак**: backpack
- **паспорт**: passport
- **пару бутылок**: a couple of bottles
- **бумажник**: wallet
- **страх**: fear
- **весь день**: the whole day
- **темно**: dark
- **прохладно**: cool
- **ужасно**: terribly
- **устал**: got tired
- **напуган**: scared
- **ночь**: night
- **очень холодной**: very cold
- **дошёл**: reached
- **шоссе**: highway
- **надеялся**: hoped
- **кто-нибудь**: someone
- **подберёт**: will pick up
- **не останавливались**: didn't stop
- **пошёл пешком**: went on foot
- **через пару часов**: in a couple of hours
- **заправки**: filling station (genitive)
- **где я**: where I am
- **вызову такси**: will call a taxi
- **отеля**: hotel (genitive)
- **пожилую**: elderly
- **заправляла**: was filling
- **спросил**: asked
- **простите, вы не подскажете**: excuse me, could you tell me
- **отвернулась**: turned back
- **села в машину**: got into the car
- **других людей**: other people (genitive)
- **та же самая**: the same
- **почему**: why
- **зашёл в здание**: entered the building
- **никакой**: no
- **вышел на улицу**: went outside

- **что происходит**: what's going on
- **услышал голос**: heard a voice
- **хочешь**: want
- **поднял глаза**: rose his eyes
- **бездомного**: homeless
- **выглядел**: looked
- **пах**: smelled (had an odor)
- **так же**: the same
- **готов**: ready
- **объяснил**: explained
- **где он находится**: where he is
- **дал номер**: gave the number
- **никто**: nobody
- **думали**: thought
- **такой как я**: like me
- **удивился**: was surprised
- **отражение**: reflection
- **ну, конечно**: well, of course
- **столько времени**: so much time
- **грязным**: dirty
- **порвана**: torn (short form)
- **плохо**: bad
- **решили, что**: decided that
- **заканчивал**: was finishing
- **оказался отличным парнем**: turned out to be a great guy
- **те**: those
- **к несчастью**: unfortunately
- **случиться**: happen
- **любой**: any
- **мне интересно**: I wonder
- **бы**: would (subjunctive mood)
- **себя повёл**: behave

Questions about the story

1. **Что Миша рассказал о людях?**
   What did Misha tell about the people?

   a. Они невежливые.
      They're not polite.

   b. Они дружелюбные.
      They're friendly.

   c. Они всегда уставшие.
      They're always tired.

   d. Они никогда не хотят разговаривать.
      They never want to talk.

2. **Миша взял в аренду навигатор. Правда или ложь?**
   Misha rented a GPS navigator. True or false?

   a. Правда.
   b. True.
   c. Ложь.
   d. False.

3. **Что произошло в пустыне?**
   What happened in the desert?

   a. Машина застряла в песке.
      The car got stuck in the sand.

   b. Сломался навигатор.
      The navigator broke down.

   c. Миша встретил ковбоя.
      Misha met a cowboy.

   d. Миша порвал одежду.
      Misha tore his clothes.

4. **Миша дошёл до заправки пешком. Правда или ложь?**
Misha went to a filling station on foot. True or false?

   a. Правда.
   b. True.
   c. Ложь.
   d. False.

5. **Почему люди на заправке не хотели его слушать?**
Why didn't people at the filling station want to listen to him?

   a. Они не понимали его.
      They didn't understand him.

   b. Он разговаривал невежливо.
      He was talking in an impolite way.

   c. Он выглядел, как бездомный.
      He looked like a homeless man.

   d. Он был не дружелюбным.
      He was unfriendly.

Answers

1. A
2. B
3. A
4. A
5. C

CHAPTER XII

Настоящий детектив — True Detective

Произошло **убийство**. Я **опытный детектив** и я **расследую** это **дело**. Я расследовал много таких дел. **Чаще всего** я работаю **один**. Моя профессия очень **опасная**. Каждый день я **рискую жизнью**. Но **работа** для меня **на первом месте**. Я верю — я могу **помочь** людям. Я **герой**.

Я приехал на **место преступления поздно вечером**. О преступлении **сообщила соседка**. Это была **красивая женщина высокого роста** с голубыми глазами. У неё были **длинные белые волосы**. **Кроме того**, она была очень **приветлива**.

Соседка услышала **крики из той квартиры около часа назад**. Затем она **сразу же вызвала полицию**.

— Ваш **сосед** жил один?

— Да, он не был **женат**.

— Вы не **замечали** ничего **странного в последнее время**?

— Юрий был очень **задумчивым**.

— Вы не видели **преступника**? — спросил я.

— **К сожалению**, нет. Но я заметила его **чёрный плащ**. Преступник бежал **вниз по лестнице**.

— Что ж, **спасибо за информацию**.

— **Не за что**. Была **рада** помочь.

Эксперты из лаборатории уже уехали. Я люблю работать один. Мне нужна **тишина**. Так **легче сосредоточиться**.

Я **вошёл** в квартиру. Я **включил свет**. Нужно было всё **внимательно осмотреть**. Нужно **быть осторожным**. **Каждая** маленькая **деталь** могла **стать уликой**. Это была обычная **двухкомнатная квартира**. **Чёрно-белые** фотографии **на стенах**. Я **заметил следы** на полу **в прихожей**. Очевидно, преступник **не снял ботинки**. В тот день на улице шёл **сильный дождь**. **Пол** был грязным. **Дверь в гостиную** была **закрыта**. Я заметил, что **дверь** в спальню **была приоткрыта**.

Самая **неприятная** вещь: я увидел **жертву**. На полу **у окна** лежал мужчина. На нём была **тёмная кофта** и **камуфляжные штаны**. **Возле** него было небольшое красное **пятно**. Я **вздрогнул**: вдруг **зазвонил телефон**. Я **снял трубку**. Это звонили из лаборатории. **В мусорном баке** за домом **нашли пистолет**.

Я **положил трубку** и услышал, что **скрипнула дверь**. Он вернулся? Я **спрятался за дверью** и слушал.

— Я дома, **малыш**, — сказал **голос** в прихожей.

— **Мамочка**! — **закричал** я.

— Ты снова **смотрел телевизор**?

— Нет, **играл с игрушками**.

— **Умничка**. Я принесла **что-то вкусное. Идём сюда**.

— Сейчас, мам. **Я мигом**.

Нет времени рассказывать дальше. Нужно **срочно** положить игрушки **на место**. Это мои любимые **кукла Барби** и **деревянный солдатик**. А **что же делать** с пятном **красной краски** на полу? **Что-нибудь придумаю**. Я же детектив.

119

Краткое содержание истории

Произошло убийство. Я опытный детектив. Я приехал на место преступления и поговорил с соседкой. Это она вызвала полицию. Она была очень красивой и приветливой. Её сосед Юрий жил один. Соседка не видела преступника. Я вошёл в квартиру, где всё случилось. Дверь в спальню была приоткрыта. Я вошёл и увидел мужчину на полу. Около него я заметил небольшое красное пятно. Зазвонил телефон. Это были эксперты. В мусорном баке за домом нашли пистолет. Вдруг скрипнула дверь. Из прихожей послышался голос. Это пришла мама. Нет времени рассказывать дальше. Нужно убрать куклу Барби, деревянного солдатика. А что делать с красным пятном краски? Придумаю. Я же детектив.

Summary of the story

A murder took place. I am an experienced detective. I arrived at the crime scene and spoke to a neighbor. She was the one who called the police. She was very beautiful and welcoming. Her neighbor Yuriy lived alone. She didn't see the criminal. I came into the apartment. It happened there. The bedroom door was ajar. I came in and saw a man lying on the floor. I noticed a little red stain next to him. The phone rang. It was the experts. There was a pistol found in the waste bin behind the building. The door suddenly creaked. I heard the voice coming from the living room. It was my mum. I don't have time to keep telling the story. I must put the Barbie doll and the toy soldier away. And what shall I do with the red color stain? I'm gonna figure it out. I told you I'm a detective.

Vocabulary

- **настоящий**: real
- **убийство**: murder
- **опытный детектив**: experienced detective
- **расследую**: investigate
- **дело**: case
- **чаще всего**: most often
- **один**: alone
- **опасная**: dangerous
- **рискую жизнью**: risk life
- **работа**: work
- **на первом месте**: in the first place
- **верю**: believe
- **помочь**: help
- **герой**: hero
- **место преступления**: crime scene
- **поздно вечером**: late in the evening
- **сообщила**: reported
- **соседка**: neighbor (female)
- **красивая женщина**: beautiful woman
- **высокого роста**: tall
- **длинные белые волосы**: long fair hair
- **кроме того**: besides

- **приветлива**: welcoming
- **крики**: screams
- **из той квартиры**: from that apartment
- **около часа назад**: about an hour ago
- **сразу же**: immediately
- **вызвала полицию**: called the police
- **сосед**: neighbor
- **женат**: married
- **замечали**: noticed
- **странного**: strange
- **в последнее время**: recently
- **задумчивым**: brooding
- **преступника**: criminal (genitive)
- **к сожалению**: unfortunately
- **чёрный плащ**: black coat
- **вниз по лестнице**: down the stairs
- **спасибо за информацию**: thank you for information
- **не за что**: not at all
- **рада**: glad

- **эксперты из лаборатории**: laboratory experts
- **тишина**: silence
- **легче**: easier
- **сосредоточиться**: focus
- **вошёл**: came into
- **включил свет**: turned on the light
- **внимательно**: attentively
- **осмотреть**: inspect
- **быть осторожным**: be careful
- **каждая**: each
- **деталь**: detail
- **стать уликой**: become evidence
- **двухкомнатная квартира**: two-room apartment
- **чёрно-белые**: black and white
- **на стенах**: on the walls
- **заметил следы**: noticed footprints
- **в прихожей**: in the hallway
- **не снял ботинки**: didn't take the shoes off
- **сильный дождь**: heavy rain

- **пол**: floor
- **дверь в гостиную**: living room door
- **закрыта**: shut (short form)
- **дверь была приоткрыта**: door was ajar
- **неприятная**: unpleasant
- **жертву**: victim (accusative)
- **у окна**: by the window
- **тёмная кофта**: dark sweatshirt
- **камуфляжные штаны**: cargo pants
- **возле**: next to
- **пятно**: stain
- **вздрогнул**: flinched
- **зазвонил телефон**: the phone rang
- **снял трубку**: answered the phone
- **в мусорном баке**: in a waste bin
- **нашли пистолет**: found a pistol
- **положил трубку**: hang up
- **скрипнула дверь**: the door creaked
- **спрятался за дверью**: hid behind the door
- **малыш**: baby
- **голос**: voice

- **мамочка**: mummy
- **закричал**: cried
- **смотрел телевизор**: watched tv
- **играл с игрушками**: played with toys
- **умничка**: good boy
- **что-то вкусное**: something delicious
- **идём сюда**: come here (imperative)
- **я мигом**: I'll be right back
- **нет времени**: no time
- **рассказывать дальше**: keep telling
- **срочно**: urgently
- **на место**: in place
- **кукла Барби**: Barbie doll
- **деревянный**: wooden
- **солдатик**: soldier
- **что же делать**: what shall I do
- **красной краски**: red paint (genitive)
- **что-нибудь придумаю**: I'm gonna figure it out

Questions about the story

1. **Профессия детектива очень опасна. Правда или ложь?**
   The profession of a detective is very dangerous. True or false?

   a. Правда.
      True.

   b. Ложь.
      False.

2. **Какое дело расследует автор?**
   Which case does the author investigate?

   a. Кражу.
      Theft.

   b. Убийство.
      Murder.

   c. Террористический акт.
      Terrorist act.

   d. Мошенничество.
      Fraud.

3. **Какой была соседка жертвы?**
   What was the victim's neighbor like?

   a. Неразговорчивой.
      Taciturn.

   b. Смешной.
      Funny.

   c. Приветливой.
      Welcoming.

   d. Грубой.
      Rude.

4. Кто звонил автору?
Who called the author?

   a. Жена.
      The wife.

   b. Соседка.
      The neighbor.

   c. Начальник.
      The boss.

   d. Эксперты из лаборатории.
      Laboratory experts.

5. Почему автор не рассказал историю до конца?
Why didn't the author tell the story till the end?

   a. Он должен убрать игрушки.
      He must put the toys in place.

   b. История слишком страшная.
      The story is too scary.

   c. У него нет времени.
      He has no time.

   d. Он не хочет раскрывать секрет.
      He doesn't want to share the secret.

Answers

1. A
2. B
3. C
4. D
5. A

CHAPTER XIII

Важный диалог — A Real Dialogue

Меня зовут Егор. Я **переводчик** и **очень люблю** свою **работу**. Я **всегда много читал**. Я с **удовольствием изучал** языки и литературу в **школе**. Я **пробовал переводить** маленькие **рассказы** с **русского** на **английский**. **Потом наоборот**. Это было моим **хобби**. **Но** хобби **стало чем-то серьёзным**.

Я **закончил университет**. У меня была **цель**: стать переводчиком. Я **начал** переводить **статьи, книги, журналы**. Переводы — моя **страсть**.

Преподаватели в университете **хвалили** меня. **Родители** мной **гордились**. Я был **уверен** в своём **будущем**. Я **сдал** все экзамены отлично. **Что дальше? Взрослая жизнь? Нужно** было **искать** работу.

Мой **город** очень **большой**. Я знал — **всё получится**. Есть много **шансов**. Я **сходил** на **одно собеседование**. Потом на **второе**. Это было **тяжело**. Моя **уверенность исчезла. Люди** были **грубыми** и **высокомерными**. Мои **оценки** за экзамены? **Опыт** — **только** это было им **интересно**.

В одном **агентстве** я **наконец получил** работу. **Низкая зарплата. Никакого отдельного кабинета. Неудобный график. Ужас.** У меня не было **выхода**. Я не **мог жить** у родителей **вечно**. Они много **сделали** для меня. **Помогли** закончить университет. **Брать** у них **деньги**? Я этого не хотел. Не мог этого **представить**.

Прошло два месяца. Это было **худшее время** в моей жизни. Мой **начальник** меня не **уважал**. Он **заставлял** меня делать его работу. Зарплата **осталась** низкой. Я был переводчиком. Это было моей **мечтой**. Что **случилось**? Я **выбрал неверный путь**?

Я **понял**, что я не уважал **себя**. Я сходил на два собеседования и **сдался**. Я был **напуган**. **Трус**. Настоящий трус. Я **привык** быть **лучше всех**. Всегда **первый**. Всегда всё **получается**. Я **встал** из-за **стола** с **документами** и пошёл в кабинет к начальнику.

— Я **увольняюсь**, — уверенно **сказал** я.
— Что, Егор? — с **улыбкой спросил** начальник.
— Вы всё **слышали**.
— Да, я слышал. Но не могу в это **поверить**. Это **смешно**. **Возвращайся** к работе. Не **говори глупостей**.
— Я говорю серьёзно. **Завтра** я не приду на работу. Я **знаю**, что я **хороший** переводчик. Я **достоин** хорошей работы и хорошего **отношения** к себе.
— **Подожди**, Егор. Я **готов повысить** тебе зарплату. **Выходные** в **субботу** и **воскресенье**. Что думаешь?
— **Всего доброго. До свидания.**

Это был **самый важный диалог** в моей жизни. **Сегодня** я **владелец** переводческого агентства. Ко мне приходят **молодые** люди. Они хотят получить хорошую работу. Перевод — их страсть. Я всегда **вспоминаю** себя. Я не **жду** опытных переводчиков. Я хочу **дать** им опыт. Нужно **отдавать**. Тогда получаешь **в два раза больше**. Я не **имею в виду** деньги.

Краткое содержание истории

Меня зовут Егор. Я переводчик. У меня была цель: стать переводчиком. Родители гордились мной, преподаватели в университете хвалили меня. Я закончил университет. Я хотел найти работу и сходил на два собеседования. Я получил работу в агентстве. Это было худшее время в моей жизни. Я много работал. Мне мало платили. Я понял, что я не уважал себя. Я испугался. Настоящий трус. Я уволился и сейчас у меня своё переводческое агентство. Я хочу дать опыт молодым людям. Нужно отдавать. Тогда получаешь в два раза больше.

Summary of the story

My name's Egor. I'm a translator. I had a goal — to become a translator. My parents were proud of me, the teachers at the university praised me. I graduated from the university. I wanted to find a job and had two job interviews. I got a job in an agency. That was the worst time of my life. I worked a lot. I was paid little. I understood I didn't respect myself. I was scared, a real coward. I quit, and now I own a translation agency. I want to give young people some experience. You must give away. You can get two times more then.

Vocabulary

- **важный диалог**: an important dialogue
- **переводчик**: translator
- **очень**: very
- **люблю**: love
- **работу**: work (accusative)
- **всегда**: always
- **много**: a lot
- **читал**: read (past form)
- **удовольствием**: pleasure (ablative)
- **изучал**: studied
- **языки**: languages
- **школе**: school (prepositional)
- **пробовал**: tried
- **переводить**: translate
- **маленькие**: little
- **рассказы**: stories
- **русского**: Russian
- **английский**: English
- **потом**: then
- **наоборот**: vice versa
- **хобби**: hobby
- **но**: but
- **стало**: became
- **чем-то**: something
- **серьёзным**: serious
- **закончил университет**: graduated from university
- **цель**: aim
- **начал**: began
- **статьи**: articles
- **книги**: books
- **журналы**: magazines
- **страсть**: pasion
- **преподаватели**: teachers
- **хвалили**: praised
- **родители**: parents
- **гордились**: were proud
- **уверен**: sure
- **будущем**: future (prepositional)
- **сдал экзамены отлично**: passed exams with flying colors
- **что дальше**: what's next
- **взрослая**: adult
- **жизнь**: life
- **нужно**: must (impersonal)
- **искать**: look for
- **город**: city
- **большой**: big
- **знал**: knew
- **всё получится**: everything will be fine
- **шансов**: chances (genitive)

- **сходил**: went
- **одно**: one
- **собеседование**: job interview
- **второе**: second
- **тяжело**: hard
- **уверенность**: confidence
- **исчезла**: disappeared
- **люди**: people
- **грубыми**: rude
- **высокомерными**: arrogant
- **оценки**: marks
- **опыт**: experience
- **только**: only
- **интересно**: interesting
- **агентстве**: agency (prepositional)
- **наконец**: finally
- **получил**: got
- **низкая**: low
- **зарплата**: salary
- **никакого отдельного кабинета**: no separate office
- **неудобный**: inconvenient
- **график**: schedule
- **ужас**: horror
- **выхода**: way out (genitive)
- **мог**: could
- **жить**: live

- **вечно**: forever
- **сделали**: did
- **помогли**: helped
- **брать**: take
- **деньги**: money
- **представить**: imagine
- **прошло два месяца**: two months passed
- **худшее время**: worst time
- **начальник**: boss
- **уважал**: respected
- **заставлял**: made
- **осталась**: remained
- **мечтой**: dream (ablative)
- **случилось**: happened
- **выбрал**: chose
- **неверный**: wrong
- **путь**: way
- **понял**: understood
- **себя**: myself
- **сдался**: gave up
- **напуган**: scared
- **трус**: coward
- **привык**: got used
- **лучше всех**: better than anyone
- **первый**: first
- **получается**: goes well
- **встал**: stood up
- **стола**: table (genitive)

131

- **документами**: documents (ablative)
- **увольняюсь**: quit
- **сказал**: said
- **улыбкой**: smile (dative)
- **спросил**: asked
- **слышали**: heard
- **поверить**: believe
- **смешно**: funny
- **возвращайся**: get back (imperative)
- **говори**: talk (imperative)
- **глупостей**: nonsense (genitive)
- **завтра**: tomorrow
- **знаю**: know
- **хороший**: good
- **достоин**: worthy of
- **отношения**: attitude (genitive)
- **подожди**: wait (imperative)
- **готов**: ready
- **повысить**: raise
- **выходные**: weekends
- **субботу**: Saturday (accusative)
- **воскресенье**: Sunday
- **всего доброго**: all the best
- **до свидания**: good bye
- **самый важный**: most important
- **диалог**: dialogue
- **сегодня**: today
- **владелец**: owner
- **молодые**: young
- **вспоминаю**: recall
- **жду**: wait
- **дать**: give
- **отдавать**: give away
- **получаешь**: get
- **в два раза больше**: two times more
- **имею в виду**: mean

Questions about the story

1. **Что Егор делал в школе?**
   What did Egor do at school?

   a. Учил стихи наизусть.
      Learned poems by heart.

   b. Переводил стихи.
      Translated poems.

   c. Переводил маленькие рассказы.
      Translated short stories.

   d. Писал рассказы.
      Wrote stories.

2. **Егор очень хорошо сдал экзамены. Правда или ложь?**
   Egor passed exams with flying colors. True or false?

   a. Правда.
      True.

   b. Ложь.
      False.

3. **Чем интересовались люди на собеседованиях?**
   What were people at job interviews interested in?

   a. Внешностью.
      Appearance.

   b. Оценками.
      Marks.

   c. Хобби.
      Hobbies.

   d. Опытом.
      Experience.

4. **Егор сказал начальнику об увольнении. Он не сразу поверил Егору. Правда или ложь?**
   Egor told the boss he was going to quit. He didn't believe Egor at once. True or false?

   a. Правда.
      True.

   b. Ложь.
      False.

5. **Кем сейчас работает Егор?**
   What is Egor now?

   a. Он писатель.
      He's a writer.

   b. Он поэт.
      He's a poet.

   c. Он художник.
      He's an artist.

   d. Он владелец переводческого агентства.
      He's the owner of a translation agency.

Answers

1. C
2. A
3. D
4. A
5. D

CHAPTER XIV

Мамина свобода — Mom's Freedom

Привет! Меня зовут Вика. У меня **трое детей**: два мальчика и одна девочка. Мои **сыновья** — **близнецы**. Им 6. Моей дочке 4. У меня есть **образование**, но сейчас я не работаю. Я **домохозяйка**.

Мне нравится моя **роль**. Я люблю **проводить время** с детьми. Люблю **заботиться о** них. Их **счастливые глаза**! Их **смех**!

Но **несколько месяцев назад** я очень **устала**.

— Мне нужно **немного отдохнуть**, — сказала я **мужу**. — Хочу немного **свободы** и **тишины**.
— **Не проблема**! — ответил он. — **В субботу** мы с детьми **поедем за город**. Останься дома. **Расслабься**.

Свобода! В субботу!

— Скажи, я **плохая мать**? — спросила я мужа.
— Почему? — **удивился** он.
— **Я рада,** что дети **уедут**. Что я буду **одна**.
— **Успокойся**! Это нормально. **Всем** нужен **отдых**.

Я **строила планы**. Что можно делать **в свободное время**? **Смотреть телевизор**? **Ходить на прогулки**? Читать книги? **Заниматься спортом**? Потом я **вспомнила**: я женщина! Я посмотрела на свои **ногти**. Кошмар! Лицо — **та же история**. О да! Я **приму ванну**, лягу на **диван**, включу **мелодраму** и буду есть пиццу. И никто не скажет мне: «Мам, **я хочу в туалет**! Мам, **дай мне кусочек**!»

Наступила суббота. Мы **позавтракали** вместе.

— Пока! Мы **будем вести себя хорошо**, — **пообещали** мальчики.

— **Не волнуйся**! **Наслаждайся**! — сказал муж и **поцеловал** меня.

Дверь закрылась. Я села в **кресло**. Тишина и свобода. Я **заказала** пиццу. **Целая** пицца **только** для меня! **Затем** я пошла в ванную. Через **пару** минут я **заметила**, что дверь **открыта**. Я **улыбнулась**. Я всегда **так делаю**. Мне нужно **слышать**, что делают дети.

— Ванна с **закрытой** дверью! **Роскошь**! — **засмеялась** я.

Теперь нужно **выбрать** фильм. Фильм, а не **мультик**! **Мелодрама**, а не **боевик**! Я **включила** телевизор.

— Мальчики, ваш любимый **сериал** про **супергероев**! — **крикнула** я и опять засмеялась. Я одна дома.

Что ж, фильм был интересным. Я посмотрела его **от начала до конца**. Без пауз. Никто не **отвлекал** меня. **Коробка** от пиццы была **пустая**. Мои ногти выглядели **прекрасно**. **Что теперь**? Я почитала **журнал**. Выпила чашку чая. И **вдруг** я поняла: я **скучаю** по детям. Я **хочу** смотреть мультики. Я хочу **играть в игры**. Я хочу читать **сказки**. Я **позвонила** мужу.

— Мы будем дома **через три часа**! **Пока**! — сказал он.

Я почитала книгу. **Просмотрела ленту** в Facebook. О, **сообщение** в WhatsApp! Я открыла его. Муж **прислал** мне **фотографии**. У них был **отличный** день! **Мороженое**, **прогулка по лесу**, игры. Они даже не скучают по мне! Я **опять** просмотрела фотографии. Они **такие милые**!

— **Ненавижу** свободу! — сказала я и **расплакалась**.

Когда муж и дети **вернулись** домой, я смотрела мультики и плакала.

— **Что случилось**? — спросил муж.

Я **обняла** их и **рассказала** о своей свободе. Они рассказали мне о своём дне. Мы **долго** смеялись. «Я **так сильно** люблю свою семью, мне не нужна свобода», — подумала я и **почувствовала**, что **засыпаю**, и вдруг...

— **Дорогая, что у нас на ужин**? — услышала я.

Краткое содержание истории

Вика мама троих детей. У неё двое сыновей-близнецов и одна дочь. Она домохозяйка. Ей нравится заботиться о детях, но она она устала. Ей нужен отдых. Муж сказал ей, что в субботу поедет с детьми за город. Она строила планы. Она хотела принять ванну, посмотреть телевизор, сделать маникюр и просто насладиться тишиной.

Вначале ей нравился её день. Она делала всё, что запланировала, но всё время вспоминала о детях. Вскоре она поняла, что скучает по ним. Она почувствовала, что ей не нужно так много свободного времени. Когда муж и дети вернулись домой, Вика плакала. Они рассказали друг другу о своём дне. Вика поняла, что очень любит свою семью. Она почти уснула, но муж спросил, что она приготовила на ужин.

Summary of the story

Vika is a mother of three children. She has two twin sons and one daughter. She's a housewife. She likes taking care of her children, but she's tired. Her husband told her he'd take the children to the country on Saturday. She made plans. She wanted to take a bath, watch TV, do her nails and just enjoy the peace and quiet.

At first, she liked her day. She did everything she'd planned to do, but she remembered her children all the time. Soon she understood she missed them. She felt she didn't need so much free time. When her husband and the children returned home Vika was crying. They told each other about how their day went. Vika understood she loves her family a lot. She was about to fall asleep, but her husband asked what she'd cooked for dinner.

Vocabulary

- **мамина свобода**: mum's freedom
- **трое детей**: three kids
- **сыновья**: sons
- **близнецы**: twins
- **образование**: education
- **домохозяйка**: housewife
- **роль**: role
- **проводить время**: spend time
- **заботиться о**: take care of
- **счастливые глаза**: happy eyes
- **смех**: laughter
- **несколько месяцев назад**: a few months ago
- **устала**: tired
- **немного отдохнуть**: have some rest
- **мужу**: husband (dative)
- **свободы**: freedom (genitive)
- **тишины**: quiet (genitive)
- **не проблема**: no problem
- **в субботу**: on Saturday
- **поедем за город**: will go to the country
- **останься**: stay (imperative)
- **расслабься**: relax (imperative)
- **плохая мать**: bad mother
- **удивился**: was surprised
- **я рада**: I'm happy/glad
- **уедут**: will leave
- **одна**: alone
- **успокойся**: calm down (imperative)
- **всем**: everybody (dative)
- **отдых**: rest
- **строила планы**: made plans
- **в свободное время**: in free time
- **смотреть телевизор**: watch TV
- **ходить на прогулки**: go for walks
- **заниматься спортом**: do sports
- **вспомнила**: remembered/recollected
- **ногти**: nails
- **кошмар**: nightmare
- **та же история**: same story
- **о**: oh
- **приму ванну**: will take a bath

- **диван:** sofa
- **мелодраму:** melodrama (accusative)
- **я хочу в туалет:** I want to the bathroom
- **дай мне:** give me (imperative)
- **кусочек:** piece
- **наступила:** came
- **позавтракали:** had breakfast
- **будем вести себя хорошо:** will behave ourselves
- **пообещали:** promised
- **не волнуйся:** don't worry (imperative)
- **наслаждайся:** enjoy (imperative)
- **поцеловал:** kissed
- **дверь:** door
- **кресло:** armchair
- **заказала:** ordered
- **целая:** whole
- **только:** only
- **затем:** then
- **пару:** a couple
- **заметила:** noticed
- **открыта:** is open
- **улыбнулась:** smiled
- **так делаю:** do so

- **слышать:** hear
- **закрытой:** closed
- **роскошь:** luxury
- **засмеялась:** laughed
- **выбрать:** choose
- **мультик:** cartoon
- **боевик:** action film
- **включила:** turned on
- **сериал:** series
- **супергероев:** super heroes (locative)
- **крикнула:** shouted
- **что ж:** well
- **от начала до конца:** from beginning till the end
- **отвлекал:** distracted
- **коробка:** box
- **пустая:** empty
- **прекрасно:** wonderful
- **что теперь:** what now
- **журнал:** magazine
- **вдруг:** suddenly
- **скучаю:** miss
- **хочу:** want
- **играть в игры:** play games
- **сказки:** fairytales
- **позвонила:** called
- **через три часа:** in three hours
- **просмотрела ленту:** looked through the feed

- **сообщение**: message
- **прислал**: sent
- **фотографии**: photos
- **отличный**: great
- **мороженое**: ice-cream
- **прогулка по лесу**: a walk in the forest
- **опять**: again
- **такие милые**: so cute
- **ненавижу**: hate
- **расплакалась**: burst out crying
- **когда**: when
- **вернулись**: returned
- **что случилось**: what's happened
- **обняла**: hugged
- **рассказала**: told
- **долго**: for a long time
- **так сильно**: so much
- **почувствовала**: felt
- **засыпаю**: falling asleep
- **дорогая**: darling
- **что у нас на ужин**: what have we got for dinner

Questions about the story

1. Сколько у Вики детей?
How many kids does Vika have?

  a. 1.
  b. 2.
  c. 4.
  d. 3.

2. У Вики нет образования. Правда или ложь?
Vika doesn't have an education. True or false?

  a. Правда.
      True.

  b. Ложь.
      False.

3. Что Вика не делала в субботу?
What did Vika not do on Saturday?

  a. Принимала ванну.
      Took a bath.

  b. Делала маникюр.
      Did her nails.

  c. Ела пиццу.
      Ate a pizza.

  d. Ходила на прогулку.
      Went for a walk.

4. Какой фильм посмотрела Вика?
What kind of film did Vika watch?

  a. Мелодраму.
      A melodrama.

b. Боевик.

An action.

c. Детектив.

A detective.

d. Мультик.

A cartoon.

5. **Вика приготовила ужин. Правда или ложь?**
Vika cooked dinner. True or false?

a. Правда.

True.

b. Ложь.

False.

Answers

1. D
2. B
3. D
4. A
5. B

CHAPTER XV

Новогоднее чудо — New Year's Miracle

Привет, меня зовут Вероника. Я **хочу рассказать** свою **историю**. Она про **Новый год** и чудо.

Это **произошло** в **прошлом году**, в **декабре**. Все **готовились** к **празднику. Город** был **белым**: везде **снег**. Улицы в ярких огнях. **Вокруг** было много **людей**. Все **спешили купить подарки** своим **родственникам** и **друзьям**.

Все мои друзья **уехали** из города. **Кто-то отмечал** праздник **за границей**, кто-то уехал к **родителям**. Мои родители **улетели** к родственникам в **Польшу**. Я не **могла** улететь с ними **из-за работы**. Я была **очень занята** в **то время. Поэтому** я **осталась одна**.

Я **всегда любила дарить** подарки. Но в **том году** я **подумала: кому** их дарить? Я была одна. **Конечно**, я подарю подарки родителям. Но это будет **после** Нового года. Это **не так интересно**. У меня не было **чувства** праздника. **Даже** новогодние **песни** не могли **помочь**.

После работы я **зашла** в **кафе**. Я **села** за **столик напротив** телевизора. **Милая официантка** принесла мой **кофе** и **пончик**.

— **Счастливого** Нового года и **Рождества**, — сказала она.
— Спасибо, **вам так же**, — **ответила** я.

Счастливые праздники? В тот **момент** я так не думала. Мне было **грустно**. **Один** день **до** Нового года. Это был мой **любимый** праздник. О нём было столько **хороших воспоминаний** из **детства**.

Я **посмотрела** на **экран** телевизора. Там **тоже** был Новый год. Он был везде. Я **начала злиться**. Но тут я **услышала что-то** о **детском доме**. Мне стало **стыдно**. Я **поняла**: это у них нет чувства праздника. Это они **одиноки**. Я не **допила** кофе, **заплатила** и **выбежала** из кафе.

Все **магазины** были **открыты**. В тот **вечер** я купила **большую сумку** подарков. Там было много **разных вещей**. Игрушки, **раскраски**, **карандаши**, **фломастеры**, **настольные игры**, **сладости, книги, свечи** и **тёплая одежда**.

Я очень хорошо **помню** тот день. Я **пришла** в детский дом и **удивилась**: я была не одна. Там было несколько **взрослых людей**. Они тоже **решили необычно** отметить праздник и помочь детям.

Как **приятно** было смотреть на счастливые **лица** детей! Они были **рады любой** вещи. Они не **ждали дорогих** подарков. Дети хотели **любви** и **внимания**. **Некоторые надели** тёплые **свитера** со **снеговиками, другие** начали **рисовать** карандашами. Один **мальчик дал** мне свой **рисунок**. Я **расплакалась**. Это был **лучший** подарок в моей **жизни**. Он **нарисовал себя** и меня. Мы **держались за руки**. **Внизу** большими **буквами** он **написал** «Спасибо за праздник».

Я много раз отмечала Новый год. Но тот праздник — самый лучший. **Сейчас** я **не только** отмечаю Новый год и Рождество с детьми. Мы **часто встречаемся**. Эти встречи всегда приносят счастье. Я **также познакомилась** с другими **волонтёрами**. Сейчас мы друзья. Эта история — моё новогоднее чудо.

Краткое содержание истории

Меня зовут Вероника. Эта история о новогоднем чуде. Я осталась одна перед Новым годом. Мои друзья и родители уехали. Мне было грустно. Украшенный город и новогодние песни не могли помочь. Я зашла в кафе и услышала о детском доме. Мне стало стыдно. Эти дети были одиноки. Я купила много подарков и отметила праздник с детьми. Один мальчик подарил мне рисунок. Он написал «Спасибо за праздник». Сейчас мы часто видимся с детьми. Также я познакомилась с другими волонтёрами. Сейчас мы друзья. Это был самый лучший праздник в моей жизни.

Summary of the story

My name's Veronika. This story is about a New Year's miracle. I was alone on New Year's Eve. My friends and parents went away. I was sad. The decorated city and New Year songs couldn't help. I went to the cafe and heard about an orphanage. I was ashamed. Those children were alone. I bought many presents and celebrated with children. One boy gave me a picture. He wrote "Thanks for the holiday". Now I often meet the children. I also met other volunteers. We're friends now. That was the best holiday in my life.

Vocabulary

- **Новогоднее чудо**: New Year's miracle
- **хочу**: want
- **рассказать**: tell
- **историю**: story (accusative)
- **Новый Год**: New Year
- **чудо**: miracle
- **произошло**: happened
- **прошлом году**: last year (prepositional)
- **декабре**: December (prepositional)
- **готовились**: were preparing
- **празднику**: holiday (dative)
- **город**: city
- **белым**: white
- **везде**: everywhere
- **снег**: snow
- **улицы**: streets
- **ярких огнях**: bright lights (ablative)
- **вокруг**: around
- **людей**: people (genitive)
- **спешили**: hurried
- **купить**: buy
- **подарки**: presents
- **родственникам**: relatives (dative)
- **друзьям**: friends (dative)
- **уехали**: gone
- **кто-то**: someone
- **отмечал**: celebrated
- **за границей**: abroad
- **родителям**: parents (dative)
- **улетели**: flew away
- **Польшу**: Poland (accusative)
- **могла**: could
- **из-за**: because of
- **работы**: work (genitive)
- **очень**: very
- **занята**: busy
- **то время**: that time
- **поэтому**: that's why
- **осталась одна**: was left alone
- **всегда**: always
- **любила**: loved
- **дарить**: give (about presents)
- **том году**: that year (prepositional)
- **подумала**: thought
- **кому**: whom

- **конечно**: of course
- **после**: after
- **не так интересно**: not that interesting
- **чувства**: feeling (genitive)
- **даже**: even
- **песни**: songs
- **помочь**: help
- **зашла**: went to
- **кафе**: cafe
- **села**: sat
- **столик**: table
- **напротив**: opposite
- **телевизора**: TV (genitive)
- **милая**: nice
- **официантка**: waitress
- **принесла**: brought
- **кофе**: coffee
- **пончик**: donut
- **счастливого**: happy
- **Рождества**: Christmas (genitive)
- **сказала**: said
- **вам также**: same to you
- **ответила**: answered
- **момент**: moment
- **грустно**: sad
- **один**: one
- **до**: till
- **любимый**: favorite
- **хороших**: good
- **воспоминаний**: memories
- **детства**: childhood (genitive)
- **посмотрела**: looked
- **экран**: screen
- **тоже**: too
- **начала**: began
- **злиться**: get angry
- **услышала**: heard
- **что-то**: something
- **детском доме**: orphanage (prepositional)
- **стыдно**: ashamed
- **поняла**: understood
- **одиноки**: lonely (short plural form)
- **допила**: finished (about a drink)
- **заплатила**: paid
- **выбежала**: ran out
- **магазины**: shops
- **открыты**: open
- **вечер**: evening
- **большую**: big
- **сумку**: bag (accusative)
- **разных**: different
- **вещей**: things (genitive)
- **игрушки**: toys
- **раскраски**: coloring books
- **карандаши**: pencils

- **фломастеры**: markers
- **настольные игры**: board games
- **сладости**: sweets
- **книги**: books
- **свечи**: candles
- **тёплая одежда**: warm clothes
- **помню**: remember
- **пришла**: came
- **удивилась**: was surprised
- **взрослых людей**: adults (genitive)
- **решили**: decided
- **необычно**: unusually
- **приятно**: pleasant
- **лица**: faces
- **рады**: glad
- **любой**: any
- **ждали**: waited
- **дорогих**: expensive
- **любви**: love (genitive)
- **внимания**: attention (genitive)
- **некоторые**: some
- **надели**: put on
- **свитера**: sweaters
- **снеговиками**: snowmen (ablative)
- **другие**: others
- **рисовать**: draw
- **мальчик**: boy
- **дал**: gave
- **рисунок**: picture
- **расплакалась**: burst out crying
- **лучший**: best
- **жизни**: life (genitive)
- **нарисовал себя**: drew himself
- **держались за руки**: held hands
- **внизу**: below
- **буквами**: letters (ablative)
- **написал**: wrote
- **сейчас**: now
- **не только**: not only
- **часто**: often
- **встречаемся**: meet
- **также**: also
- **познакомилась**: got acquainted
- **волонтёрами**: volunteers (ablative)

Questions about the story

1. Вероника рассказывает историю о...
    Veronika tells the story about...

    a. Родителях.
        Parents.

    b. Родственниках.
        Relatives.

    c. Чуде.
        A miracle.

    d. Друзьях.
        Friends.

2. Вероника любит Новый год. Но её любимый праздник —
    день рождения. Правда или ложь?
    **Veronika likes New Year. But her favorite holiday is her
    birthday. True or false?**

    a. Правда.
        True.

    b. Ложь.
        False.

3. Куда зашла Вероника после работы?
    Where did Veronika go after work?

    a. В бар.
        To the bar.

    b. В магазин.
        To the shop.

    c. В кафе.
        To the cafe.

d. В ресторан.
   To the restaurant.

4. **Вероника купила детям подарки. Какой подарок лишний?**

   Veronika bought children some presents. Which present is the odd one?

   a. Цветы.
      Flowers.

   b. Раскраска.
      A coloring book.

   c. Карандаши.
      Pencils.

   d. Книги.
      Books.

5. **Вероника отметила следующий Новый год за границей. Правда или ложь?**

   Veronika celebrated the next New Year abroad. True or false?

   a. Правда.
      True.

   b. Ложь.
      False.

Answers

1. C
2. B
3. C
4. A
5. B

CHAPTER XVI

Чехов — Chekhov

Антон Павлович Чехов — **знаменитый** русский **писатель**. Он писал на **разные темы**, но не **любил** писать о **себе**. **Автор** написал **более** 500 **произведений**. Они знамениты в России. Они знамениты **за рубежом**.

Родина Антона Павловича — **город Таганрог**. Писатель **родился** в **большой семье**. У **родителей** было **шестеро детей**. Чехов был **третьим**. Его **отец** был **купцом**. **Мать учила** детей **уважать** и **поддерживать слабых, любить** людей и **природу**. Сам Антон Павлович **говорил**: «Талант у меня от отца, а **душа** от матери».

Атмосфера в доме писателя была **строгой**. **После школы** дети **помогали** отцу.

После школы Чехов **поступил на медицинский факультет** в Москве. Он был **студентом**, но **лечил больных**. **Во время учёбы** он писал рассказы. У него было много **смешных псевдонимов**. В 1885 году Чехов был **популярным** автором **коротких рассказов**.

В 1890 году Чехов **поехал** на **остров Сахалин**. Он **хотел исследовать жизнь** в русских **тюрьмах**. Чехов **провёл перепись населения** на острове. Это была **трудная** работа. Писатель **заполнил** 10 000 **карточек**!

После Сахалина Антон Павлович **вернулся** в Москву. Тогда он был знаменитым автором и **общался** с **другими** писателями.

В 1890 году Антон Чехов **снова путешествовал**. Он поехал в **Западную Европу**. Писатель **побывал** в **Вене, Болонье, Венеции**, в **Париже** и других городах. В **Неаполе** он **поднимался** на **Везувий**!

Позже Чехов **купил** дом в **Мелихове, недалеко** от Москвы. Там он **открыл** медицинский **пункт, построил три** школы и **колокольню**, помогал **прокладывать дорогу** и лечил больных. Там он написал свои самые известные произведения. Например, **пьесу «Чайка»** и **повесть «Палата № 6»**.

Он **переехал** на **юг**, в **Ялту**. Писатель болел **туберкулёзом**. **Тёплый климат** мог ему помочь. Даже там он лечил больных. В то время он **познакомился** со своей **будущей женой, актрисой Ольгой Книппер**. В 1901 году они **поженились**. Она работала в московском **театре. Поэтому** любовь Чехов **выражал** в **письмах**. Они отправили **друг другу** более 800 писем и **телеграм**!

Последним произведением Чехова стала пьеса «**Вишнёвый сад**». **Летом** 1904 года он отправился в **Германию** лечить **лёгкие**. Антон Павлович **первый раз** в жизни **сам попросил позвать доктора**.

Чехов был **удивительным** человеком. Писатель **прожил** жизнь **не зря**.

Краткое содержание истории

Антон Павлович Чехов — известный русский писатель. Он родился в большой семье. Детям нельзя было бездельничать. Отец писателя был купцом. Чехов поступил на медицинский факультет. Всю жизнь он писал и лечил больных. Чехов много путешествовал. Он даже ездил на остров Сахалин. Писатель женился на актрисе Ольге Книппер. К сожалению, Чехов был болен туберкулёзом. Он умер в Германии. Он написал много известных произведений. Например, «Вишнёвый сад» и «Чайка».

Summary of the story

Anton Pavlovich Chekhov is a famous Russian writer. He was born in a big family. Children weren't allowed to do nothing. His father was a merchant. Family moved to Moscow. He enrolled in medical school. He had been writing and curing the sick for all his life. Chekhov traveled a lot. He even visited Sakhalin Island.The writer married an actress, Olga Knipper. Unfortunately, Chekhov had tuberculosis. He died in Germany. He wrote many famous works. For example "The Cherry Orchard", "The Seagull".

Vocabulary

- **Антон Павлович Чехов**: Anton Pavlovich Chekhov
- **полна**: full (short form)
- **интересных**: interesting
- **фактов**: facts (genitive plural)
- **знаменитый**: famous
- **писатель**: writer
- **разные**: different
- **темы**: topics
- **любил**: liked
- **себе**: himself
- **автор**: author
- **более**: more
- **произведений**: works (genitive)
- **за рубежом**: abroad
- **родина**: homeland
- **город**: city
- **Таганрог**: Taganrog
- **родился**: was born
- **большой**: big
- **семье**: family (prepositional)
- **родителей**: parents (genitive)
- **шестеро детей**: six children
- **третьим**: third
- **отец**: father
- **купцом**: merchant (ablative)
- **мать**: mother
- **учила**: taught
- **уважать**: respect
- **поддерживать**: support
- **слабых**: the weak (genitive)
- **любить**: love
- **природу**: nature (accusative)
- **говорил**: said
- **душа**: soul
- **атмосфера**: atmosphere
- **строгой**: strict
- **после школы**: after school
- **помогали**: helped
- **поступил на медицинский факультет**: enrolled in a medical school
- **студентом**: student (ablative)
- **лечил больных**: cured the sick
- **во время учёбы**: during the studies

- **смешных псевдонимов**: funny pseudonyms (genitive)
- **популярным**: popular
- **коротких**: short
- **рассказов**: stories (genitive)
- **поехал**: went
- **остров Сахалин**: Sakhalin Island
- **хотел**: wanted
- **исследовать**: explore
- **жизнь**: life
- **тюрьмах**: prisons (prepositional)
- **провёл перепись населения**: conducted population census
- **трудная**: hard
- **заполнил**: filled in
- **карточек**: cards (genitive)
- **вернулся**: came back
- **общался**: communicated
- **другими**: other
- **снова**: again
- **путешествовал**: traveled
- **Западную Европу**: Western Europe (accusative)
- **побывал**: visited
- **Вене**: Vienna (prepositional)
- **Болонье**: Bologna (prepositional)
- **Венеции**: Venice (prepositional)
- **Париже**: Paris (prepositional)
- **Неаполе**: Naples (prepositional)
- **поднимался**: climbed
- **Везувий**: Vesuvius
- **купил**: bought
- **Мелихове**: Melikhovo (prepositional)
- **недалеко**: not far
- **открыл**: opened
- **пункт**: post
- **построил**: built
- **три**: three
- **колокольню**: bell tower (accusative)
- **прокладывать дорогу**: build a road
- **пьесу**: play (accusative)
- **«Чайка»**: "The Seagull"
- **повесть**: narrative
- **«Палата № 6»**: "Ward № 6"
- **переехал**: moved
- **юг**: south

- **Ялту**: Yalta (accusative)
- **туберкулёзом**: tuberculosis (ablative)
- **тёплый климат**: warm climate
- **познакомился**: got acquainted
- **будущей женой**: future wife (ablative)
- **актрисой**: actress (ablative)
- **Ольгой Книппер**: Olga Knipper (ablative)
- **поженились**: got married
- **театре**: theatre (prepositional)
- **поэтому**: that's why
- **выражал**: expressed
- **письмах**: letters (prepositional)
- **друг другу**: each other
- **телеграмм**: telegrams (genitive)
- **последним**: last
- **«Вишнёвый сад»**: "The Cherry Orchard"
- **летом**: in summer
- **Германию**: Germany (accusative)
- **лёгкие**: lungs
- **первый раз**: first time
- **сам**: himself
- **попросил**: asked
- **позвать**: call
- **доктора**: doctor (accusative)
- **удивительным**: amazing
- **прожил**: lived
- **не зря**: not in vain

Questions about the story

1. **Кем работал отец Чехова?**
    What was Chekhov's father?

    a. Купцом.
        Merchant.

    b. Писателем.
        Writer.

    c. Врачом.
        Doctor.

    d. Портным.
        Tailor.

2. **Что делали дети после школы?**
    What did children do after school?

    a. Делали домашнее задание.
        Did homework.

    b. Играли в игры.
        Played games.

    c. Помогали отцу.
        Helped the father.

    d. Изучали медицину.
        Studied medicine.

3. **Сколько школ построил Чехов в Мелихове?**
    How many schools did Chekhov build in Melikhovo?

    a. Одну.
        One.

    b. Пять.
        Five.

c. Четыре.
Four.

d. Три.
Three.

4. **Чехов очень часто виделся с Ольгой Книппер. Правда или ложь?**
Chekhov often met Olga Knipper. True or false?

a. Правда.
True.

b. Ложь.
False.

5. **Чехов всегда звал доктора при болезни. Правда или ложь?**
Chekhov always called the doctor being ill. True or false?

a. Правда.
True.

b. Ложь.
False.

Answers

1. A
2. C
3. D
4. B
5. B

CHAPTER XVII

Мечта — A Dream

Семья — моё **любимое слово**. Я всегда **мечтала** о **свадьбе**. **Даже** в **детском саду**. На **Рождество** все **дети** были **зайцами**, **кроликами**, **принцессами**, **медведями**, **щенками** или **котятами**. Я **хотела** быть **невестой**. Это была моя мечта. **Мама** и **папа** даже **переживали**.

Мои **родители** — **лучшая пара в мире**. Они **очень сильно любят друг друга**. Да, **иногда** они **ссорятся**. **Какие отношения идеальны**? Они для меня **пример**. Они всегда **говорили**: отношения не **простая вещь**. **Бывают разные проблемы**. Есть разные **ситуации**.

Я была **готова к трудностям**. **Бог дал** мне **шанс**. Я **встретила мужчину**. Его зовут Паша. Он **профессиональный фотограф**. Мы **познакомились** на свадьбе моей **подруги Иры**. Он **сделал** фотографии.

— Я **влюбился** в тебя, Лера. Ты была **такой красивой** на фото. Я **позвонил** Ире и **спросил** твой **номер телефона**, — **часто** говорил он **позже**.

— **Правда?** — не **могла поверить** я.

Мы **проводим много времени** вместе. У нас **одинаковые хобби** и **интересы: книги**, **кино**, **музыка**, **искусство**.

В **прошлом месяце** мы хотели **навестить** моих родителей. **К сожалению**, Паша **был занят**. В **сентябре** всегда **много дел**. Я

164

поехала **одна**. Родители **ждали** нас **обоих**. Они **немного** **расстроились**. Им очень **нравился** Паша. Папа **любил** **поговорить** с моим **парнем** о **машинах** и о **политике**. Мама **обсуждала** с ним **новые** фильмы, готовила **вкусный пирог** и чай.

На **следующий день** Паша **поздно вернулся** с работы.

— Хочешь **кушать**? — **спросила** я.
— Нет, **спасибо, Лера**, — **ответил** он.
— Ты **устал**?
— Немного. **Не переживай**.
— **Хорошо**.

Это было **странно**. Я переживала. **Что случилось**? Я **начала** **думать**. Со мной **что-то не так**? Я его **обидела**?

Я **проснулась ночью**. Я **услышала** Пашин **голос**. Он разговаривал по телефону. В **ванной комнате**. **Почему**? Я услышала слово «люблю». **Не может быть**! Паша меня не любит. У него есть **другая девушка**. **Измена**! Моя мечта была **мертва**. Я **ничего** не сказала Паше. **Через десят минут** он вернулся и **уснул**.

Это были **выходные**. Паша **снова** встал ночью. Я не могла **успокоиться**.

— Паша, что ты делаешь? **Сейчас пять часов**, — сказала я.
— Я **знаю**. Я хотел тебя **разбудить** через **несколько** минут.
— **Что**? **Зачем**?
— Это **секрет**. **Оденься тепло**.

Мы **сели в машину**. **Вокруг** был **туман**. Мы приехали к **озеру возле леса**. Было очень **красиво**. Это был **рассвет**.

Мы вышли из машины. Я пошла **вперёд**. **Вдруг** я услышала музыку. Из леса вышли **музыканты**. Они играли нашу любимую **песню**. Паша подошёл ко мне и **обнял**. **Затем** он **встал на одно колено**.

— Любимая, ты выйдешь за меня?

— Ох... Да, **конечно** да!

Какой сюрприз! Я **поняла**: **всё это время** Паша **готовился сделать предложение**. «Люблю» он говорил **обо** мне. Зачем я переживала? Паша — лучший мужчина в мире. С ним моя **мечта сбылась**!

Краткое содержание истории

Я всегда мечтала о семье. Мои родители — лучшая пара в мире. Бог дал мне шанс: я встретила Пашу. Мы проводим много времени вместе. Однажды Паша не смог навестить моих родителей. Я поехала одна. Родители немного расстроились. Затем Паша поздно пришёл с работы. Я переживала. Однажды он встал ночью и говорил по телефону. Вдруг он меня не любит? Он снова встал ночью и я хотела с ним поговорить. Но мы куда-то поехали на машине. Это был сюрприз. Мы приехали в лес. Музыканты играли нашу любимую песню. Паша сделал мне предложение. Он лучший мужчина в мире.

Summary of the story

I've always dreamed about having a family. My parents are the best couple in the world. God gave me a chance: I met Pasha. We spend a lot of time together. One day Pasha couldn't visit my parents. I went alone. The parents were a bit disappointed. Then Pasha came home late after work. I was worried. Once, he woke up at night and spoke on the phone. What if he doesn't love me? He woke up at night again, and I wanted to talk to him. But we went somewhere by car. We came to a forest. Musicians were playing our favorite song. That was a surprise. Pasha proposed to me. He's the best man in the world.

Vocabulary

- **мечта**: dream
- **семья**: family
- **любимое слово**: favorite word
- **всегда**: always
- **мечтала**: dreamed
- **свадьбе**: wedding (prepositional)
- **даже**: even
- **детском саду**: kindergarten (prepositional)
- **Рождество**: Christmas
- **дети**: children
- **зайцами**: hares (ablative)
- **кроликами**: rabbits (ablative)
- **принцессами**: princesses (ablative)
- **медведями**: bears (ablative)
- **щенками**: puppies (ablative)
- **котятами**: kittens (ablative)
- **хотела**: wanted
- **невестой**: bride (ablative)
- **мама**: mother
- **папа**: father
- **переживали**: were worried
- **родители**: parents
- **лучшая пара в мире**: best couple in the world
- **очень сильно любят друг друга**: love each other very much
- **иногда**: sometimes
- **ссорятся**: argue
- **какие**: which
- **отношения**: relationship
- **идеальны**: perfect (short form)
- **пример**: example
- **говорили**: told
- **простая вещь**: simple thing
- **бывают разные проблемы**: there are different problems
- **ситуации**: situations
- **готова к трудностям**: ready for hardships
- **Бог**: God
- **дал**: gave
- **шанс**: chance
- **встретила**: met

- **мужчину**: man (accusative)
- **профессиональный**: professional
- **фотограф**: photographer
- **познакомились**: got acquainted
- **подруги**: friend (female, genitive)
- **Иры**: Ira (genitive)
- **сделал**: made
- **влюбился**: fell in love
- **такой красивой**: so beautiful
- **позвонил**: called
- **спросил**: asked
- **номер телефона**: phone number
- **часто**: often
- **позже**: later
- **правда**: really
- **могла поверить**: could believe
- **проводим много времени вместе**: spend much time together
- **одинаковые**: same
- **хобби**: hobbies
- **интересы**: interests
- **книги**: books
- **кино**: films
- **музыка**: music
- **искусство**: art
- **прошлом месяце**: last month (prepositional)
- **навестить**: visit
- **к сожалению**: unfortunately
- **был занят**: was busy
- **сентябре**: September (prepositional)
- **много дел**: lots to do
- **одна**: alone
- **ждали**: waited
- **обоих**: both
- **немного**: a bit
- **расстроились**: got disappointed
- **нравился**: liked
- **любил поговорить**: loved talking
- **парнем**: boyfriend (ablative)
- **машинах**: cars (prepositional)
- **политике**: politics (prepositional)
- **обсуждала**: discussed
- **новые**: new
- **вкусный пирог**: delicious pie
- **чай**: tea

- **следующий день**: next day
- **поздно вернулся**: came back late
- **кушать**: eat
- **спросила**: asked
- **спасибо**: thanks
- **ответил**: answered
- **устал**: got tired
- **не переживай**: don't worry (imperative)
- **хорошо**: ok
- **странно**: strange
- **что случилось**: what happened
- **начала думать**: began thinking
- **что-то не так**: something's wrong
- **обидела**: offended
- **проснулась**: woke up
- **ночью**: at night
- **услышала**: heard
- **голос**: voice
- **ванной комнате**: bathroom (prepositional)
- **почему**: why
- **не может быть**: can't be
- **другая девушка**: another girl
- **измена**: adultery

- **мертва**: dead (short form)
- **ничего**: nothing
- **через десять минут**: in ten minutes
- **уснул**: fell asleep
- **выходные**: weekend
- **снова**: again
- **успокоиться**: calm down
- **сейчас**: now
- **пять часов**: five o'clock
- **знаю**: know
- **разбудить**: wake
- **несколько**: several
- **что**: what
- **зачем**: what for
- **секрет**: secret
- **оденься тепло**: get dressed in warm clothes (imperative)
- **сели в машину**: got into the car
- **вокруг**: around
- **туман**: fog
- **озеру**: lake (dative)
- **возле леса**: near a forest
- **красиво**: beautiful
- **рассвет**: dawn
- **вперёд**: ahead
- **вдруг**: suddenly
- **музыканты**: musicians
- **песню**: song (accusative)

- **обнял**: hugged
- **затем**: then
- **встал на одно колено**: knelt down
- **любимая**: sweetheart
- **ты выйдешь за меня**: will you marry me
- **конечно**: of course
- **какой сюрприз**: what a surprise
- **поняла**: understood
- **всё это время**: all of that time
- **готовился**: had been preparing
- **сделать предложение**: propose
- **обо**: about
- **мечта сбылась**: dream came true

Questions about the story

1. **Лера всегда мечтала о...**
   Lera has always dreamed of...

   a. Свадьбе.
      A wedding.

   b. Путешествии.
      A trip.

   c. Дружбе.
      Friendship.

   d. Карьере.
      Career.

2. **Родители Леры часто ссорились. Правда или ложь?**
   Lera's parents often argued. True or false?

   a. Правда.
      True.

   b. Ложь.
      False.

3. **Где познакомились Лера и Паша?**
   Where did Lera and Pasha meet?

   a. На вечеринке.
      At a party.

   b. В кафе.
      At a cafe.

   c. В кино.
      At the cinema.

   d. На свадьбе.
      At a wedding.

4. **Почему Паша не навестил родителей Леры?**
    Why didn't Pasha visit Lera's parents?

    a. Он заболел.
        He fell ill.

    b. Он уехал.
        He went away.

    c. У него было много дел.
        He had lots to do.

    d. Он забыл о встрече.
        He forgot about the meeting.

5. **Где Паша сделал Лере предложение?**
    Where did Pasha propose to Lera?

    a. У океана.
        By the ocean.

    b. У реки.
        By the river.

    c. У озера.
        By the lake.

    d. В саду.
        By the garden.

Answers

1. A
2. B
3. D
4. C
5. C

CHAPTER XVIII

Свободное место — An Empty Seat

Эту историю мне **рассказала подруга** Лена. Она **произошла около года назад**. Она **ждала ребёнка. Конечно же**, она часто **посещала врачей**. Обычно **в больницу** её **возил муж**. Но **в тот день** он был **в командировке**. Лене **пришлось** ехать **на общественном транспорте**.

Это был **дождливый** день. **Поздняя осень**. Лена долго **ждала на остановке**. Она очень **устала стоять**. У неё **болели ноги**. Болела **спина**. Но **сесть** она **не могла**: скамейка была **холодная** и **сырая**. «**Отлично**, — подумала Лена, — Я **обязательно простужусь**».

Наконец, **пришёл** её **трамвай**. Он был **набит людьми**. «До больницы около **сорока минут**, — **считала** Лена. — Сорок минут **на ногах**!»

Она зашла в трамвай. **Чудо**! Свободное место! **Только одно**! Лена села. **Какое облегчение**! Она **расслабилась**, закрыла глаза. **Следующая** остановка. Вошёл **пожилой мужчина**. Лена **внимательно** посмотрела на него. Она **заметила несколько медалей** у него **на груди**.

«Должно быть, **ветеран войны**», — подумала она.

Было ясно: ему **тяжело** стоять. Лена посмотрела на людей **вокруг**. Никто не замечал его. Или они **просто делали вид**? Лена **хотела встать** и сказать:

— **Эй, люди**! Этот человек **отдал** свою **молодость ради мира**! Ради вас! **Уступите ему место**!

Но они все **видели** мужчину. Они были просто **безразличные**. Моя подруга встала и сказала мужчине:

— Садитесь, пожалуйста!

Мужчина был **рад**. Он **поблагодарил** Лену и сел на её место. Но **через секунду** он быстро встал.

— Нет, нет! **Я не могу**! Я просто **не заметил**! **Не обижайте меня**. Я не могу сидеть, когда **беременная** женщина стоит.

Лена хотела **возразить**. Да, она беременная, но она не **больная**. Она **молодая**, **сильная** женщина. Она **оглянулась: никто не собирался** вставать. Она хотела сесть, но **услышала голос**:

— **Дедушка, идите сюда**! Садитесь на моё место.

Лена **оглянулась**. **Молодой** человек **дружелюбно** смотрел на неё и на мужчину. Он **улыбался**. **Почти смеялся**.

«**Что смешного**?» — подумала Лена.

Она села на своё место. Пожилой мужчина сел на место молодого человека. Молодой человек стоял и **держался за поручень одной рукой**. Одной рукой... Лена заметила, что **левый рукав** его **куртки** был **пустой**. У молодого человека не было левой руки!

Он **понял**, что Лена заметила это и **засмеялся**. Лена засмеялась **в ответ**. Пожилой мужчина **тоже** всё понял. И тоже засмеялся. Они смеялись и смотрели **друг на друга**. **Слова** были **лишними**. А пассажиры смотрели в свои **телефоны** и **газеты**. Им было **стыдно? Не знаю**.

Кстати, Лена в тот день не простудилась.

Краткое содержание истории

Подругу рассказчика зовут Лена. Эта история произошла с ней около года назад. Лена ждала ребёнка. Она часто посещала врачей. В тот день она ехала в больницу на трамвае. Она очень устала. В трамвае было очень много людей. Но Лена нашла свободное место. Вскоре в трамвай зашёл пожилой мужчина. Ветеран войны.

Никто не уступил ему место. Лена предложила ему сесть. Мужчина согласился. Затем он заметил, что Лена беременна. Он сказал ей садиться снова. Какой-то молодой человек уступил ему своё место. Он смеялся и улыбался. Лена заметила, что у него нет одной руки. Лена, пожилой мужчина и молодой человек смотрели друг на друга и смеялись.

Summary of the story

The narrator's friend is Lena. The story happened to her about a year ago. Lena was expecting a baby. She used to visit the doctor often. That day she was going to hospital by tram. She was very tired. There were lots of people on the tram. However, Lena found a vacant seat. Soon an elderly man got on the tram. A war veteran.

Nobody yielded their seat to him. Lena offered him a seat. The man agreed. Then he noticed Lena was pregnant. He told her to sit down again. Some young man yielded his seat to him. He was laughing and smiling. Lena noticed he didn't have one hand. Lena, the elderly man and the young man were looking at each other and laughing.

Vocabulary

- **свободное место**: vacant seat
- **рассказала**: told
- **подруга**: friend (female)
- **произошла**: happened
- **около года назад**: about a year ago
- **ждала ребёнка**: was expecting a baby
- **конечно же**: of course
- **посещала врачей**: was attending doctors
- **в больницу**: to hospital
- **возил**: took (by vehicle)
- **муж**: husband
- **в тот день**: that day
- **в командировке**: on business trip
- **пришлось**: had to
- **на общественном транспорте**: by public transport
- **дождливый**: rainy
- **поздняя осень**: late autumn
- **ждала на остановке**: was waiting at the stop
- **устала стоять**: was tired of standing
- **болели ноги**: feet hurt
- **спина**: back
- **сесть**: sit down
- **не могла**: couldn't
- **скамейка**: bench
- **холодная**: cold
- **сырая**: damp
- **отлично**: great
- **обязательно простужусь**: will surely catch a cold
- **пришёл**: arrived
- **трамвай**: tram
- **набит людьми**: packed with people
- **около сорока минут**: about forty minutes
- **считала**: was counting
- **на ногах**: on feet
- **чудо**: miracle
- **только одно**: only one
- **какое облегчение**: what a relief
- **расслабилась**: relaxed
- **закрыла**: closed
- **следующая**: next
- **пожилой**: elderly
- **мужчина**: man
- **внимательно**: attentively
- **заметила**: noticed

- **несколько медалей**: a few medals
- **на груди**: on chest
- **ветеран войны**: war veteran
- **было ясно**: it was clear
- **тяжело**: hard
- **вокруг**: around
- **просто**: just
- **делали вид**: were pretending
- **хотела встать**: wanted to get up
- **эй, люди**: hey, people
- **отдал**: gave
- **молодость**: youth
- **ради**: for the sake of
- **мира**: peace (genitive)
- **уступите ему место**: yield a seat to him (imperative)
- **видели**: saw
- **безразличные**: indifferent
- **рад**: glad
- **поблагодарил**: thanked
- **через секунду**: in a second
- **я не могу**: I can't
- **не заметил**: didn't notice
- **не обижайте меня**: don't offend me (imperative)
- **беременная**: pregnant
- **возразить**: object
- **больная**: sick
- **молодая**: young
- **сильная**: strong
- **оглянулась**: looked around
- **не собирался**: wasn't going to
- **услышала голос**: heard a voice
- **дедушка**: grandpa (a form of address to an old man)
- **идите сюда**: come here
- **оглянулась**: looked around
- **young**: молодой
- **дружелюбно**: in a friendly way
- **улыбался**: was smiling
- **почти смеялся**: was almost laughing
- **что смешного**: what's so funny
- **держался за поручень**: was holding on a handrail
- **одной рукой**: with one hand
- **левый**: left
- **рукав**: sleeve
- **куртки**: jacket (genitive)
- **пустой**: empty

- **понял**: understood
- **что**: that
- **засмеялся**: laughed out loud
- **в ответ**: in reply
- **тоже**: as well
- **друг на друга**: at each other
- **слова**: words
- **лишними**: superfluous
- **телефоны**: phones
- **газеты**: newspapers
- **стыдно**: ashamed
- **не знаю**: I don't know
- **кстати**: by the way

Questions about the story

1. **Почему Лена поехала в больницу на общественном транспорте?**
   Why did Lena go to hospital by public transport?

   a. У неё не было машины.
      She didn't have a car.

   b. Она не умеет водить.
      She can't drive.

   c. Она не знала дороги.
      She didn't know the way.

   d. Её муж был в командировке.
      Her husband was on a business trip.

2. **Лена отлично себя чувствовала. Правда или ложь?**
   Lena felt great. True or false?

   a. Правда.
      True.

   b. Ложь.
      False.

3. **Кому Лена уступила место?**
   Who did Lena yield her seat to?

   a. Другой беременной женщине.
      Another pregnant woman.

   b. Молодому человеку.
      A young man.

   c. Пожилому мужчине.
      An elderly man.

d. Ребёнку.
   A child.

4. Кто уступил место ветерану войны?
   Who yielded the seat to the war veteran?

   a. Больная женщина.
      A sick woman.

   b. Ребёнок.
      A child.

   c. Молодой человек без руки.
      A young man without a hand.

   d. Пожилая женщина.
      An elderly woman.

5. Что делали другие пассажиры?
   What were the other passengers doing?

   a. Смеялись.
      Laughing.

   b. Улыбались.
      Smiling.

   c. Им стало стыдно.
      They were ashamed.

   d. Смотрели в телефоны и газеты.
      Were staring at their phones and newspapers.

Answers

1. D
2. B
3. C
4. C
5. D

CHAPTER XIX

Выбор — A Choice

У меня есть **подруга**. Её зовут Аня. Мы дружим **с раннего детства**. Эта **история** о её профессии.

В школе она **мечтала** стать **художницей**.

«**Искусство** — это не профессия, — говорили её **родители**. — **Когда** ты **станешь старше**, ты это **поймешь**».

Аня становилась старше и любила искусство **ещё больше**. Она ходила в **художественную школу**. Много **рисовала**. **Читала** книги о **знаменитых** художниках. Ходила на **выставки**.

Аня **хорошо училась** в школе. Она **интересовалась** математикой и литературой. **После** школы она хотела **поступать** в **Академию искусств**. Но её папа сказал:

— **Если** ты это сделаешь, я не буду **платить за** твоё **обучение**. Я не буду платить за твоё **жильё**. Я не буду **давать** тебе деньги.

Анин папа был **строгим**. Она **знала**, что он говорит **правду**. Она знала, что мама **поддерживает** папу. И она **сделала свой выбор**. Нет, она не стала **адвокатом** или **врачом**. Она поступила в Академию! Её **обучение** было **бесплатным**.

Днём она училась, а **ночью** работала **официанткой**. Этих денег было **достаточно**, чтобы платить за жильё и **покупать еду**. Никаких **ночных клубов** и **путешествий**. Я и наши друзья **помогали** ей. Нам было очень **жаль** Аню. Но она всегда выглядела **счастливой**. Никогда не **жаловалась**. Её любовь к искусству была **сильнее** этих **трудностей**.

Аня очень **хорошо училась**. Все **хвалили** её. Она **участвовала в конкурсах** и выставках. Она **надеялась**, что кто-нибудь **заметит** её талант. **А ещё... Что** папа **поймёт** её.

Кстати, папа был очень **удивлён**. Он **не думал**, что Аня **откажется** от его помощи и денег. Он не понимал свою дочь. Он не знал: она **сильная**. Он **был уверен**, что она **бросит** Академию и искусство.

Этого **не произошло**. Аня окончила **первый курс**. Начались **каникулы**. Она не хотела **проводить** их дома. Я поддержала её, и мы **всё лето провели** на **даче** моих родителей. Мы **купались**, **загорали** и просто **наслаждались** жизнью. **Конечно же**, Аня много рисовала. Каждый день.

На втором курсе Аня **нашла** работу в **детской** художественной школе. Она не **зарабатывала больше**, но работа была **связана** с искусством. Дети **обожали** её, а она обожала их. Мне **кажется**, они **чувствовали** — она любит их и эту работу.

На третьем курсе мы помогли Ане **организовать свою собственную** выставку. Она было **довольно успешной**.

Успех! Приглашения, выставки! Даже **за границей**. Она **доказала** родителям, что искусство — это профессия, и она **приносит** деньги! И её папа **признал** это.

Все думали, что Аня счастлива, но не я. Её **улыбка** была **грустной**. Её **глаза** были грустными. Её **новые картины** были грустными. **Однажды** я спросила её:

— **Что случилось**?
— Я **скучаю** по школе, — ответила она. — Я **успешная**, но **такая жизнь — не для меня**.

В тот вечер Аня сделала **ещё один** выбор. Она **решила открыть** свою детскую художественную школу. Её родители **снова** не поняли её. **Учить** детей? Она могла **стать знаменитой**!

А я поддержала свою подругу. Она счастлива и **делает** счастливыми **других людей.**

Краткое содержание истории

Аня с детства хотела стать художницей. Её родители не одобряли этот выбор. Они были уверены, что искусство не может быть профессией. Они надеялись, что Аня вырастет и выберет что-то другое. Но Аня решила поступать в Академию искусств. Её отец отказался помогать ей финансово. Он думал, что она испугается и изменит своё решение.

Однако Аня поступила в Академию. Она училась и работала официанткой. Девушка много рисовала. Позже она нашла работу в детской художественной школе. Через несколько лет она стала успешной художницей. Её родители признали свою ошибку. Но Аня не была счастлива. Она скучала по школе. Девушка бросила карьеру и открыла свою художественную школу для детей. Родители снова не поняли её. Но это уже не важно.

Summary of the story

Ann has wanted to be a painter since childhood. Her parents didn't approve of this choice. They didn't believe art is an actual profession. They hoped that Ann would grow up and choose something else. However, Ann decided to enter an art academy. Her father refused to support her financially. He thought she would get scared and change her decision.

Even so, Ann entered the academy. She studied and worked as a waitress. Ann painted a lot. Later she found a job in a children's art school. In a few years, she became a successful painter. Her parents admitted to their mistake. But Ann wasn't happy. She missed the school. The girl gave up her career and opened her own art school for children. Her parents still didn't understand her. But it didn't matter anymore.

Vocabulary

- **подруга**: friend (female)
- **с раннего детства**: since early childhood
- **история**: story
- **в школе**: at school
- **мечтала**: dreamed
- **художницей**: painter (ablative, feminine)
- **искусство**: art
- **родители**: parents
- **когда**: when
- **станешь старше**: will get older
- **поймешь**: will understand
- **ещё больше**: still more
- **художественную школу**: art school (accusative)
- **рисовала**: painted
- **читала**: read
- **знаменитых**: famous
- **выставки**: exhibitions
- **хорошо училась**: did well
- **интересовалась**: was interested
- **после**: after
- **поступать в академию искусств**: enter art academy
- **если**: if

- **платить за**: pay for
- **обучение**: studies
- **жильё**: accommodation
- **давать**: give
- **знала**: knew
- **строгим**: strict
- **правду**: the truth (accusative)
- **поддерживает**: supports
- **сделала свой выбор**: made her choice
- **адвокатом**: lawyer (ablative)
- **врачом**: doctor (ablative)
- **обучение**: studies
- **бесплатным**: free
- **днём**: at day
- **ночью**: at night
- **официанткой**: waitress (ablative)
- **достаточно**: enough
- **покупать еду**: buy food
- **ночных клубов**: night clubs (genitive)
- **путешествий**: trips (genitive plural)
- **помогали**: helped
- **жаль**: sorry for

- **выглядела счастливой**: looked happy
- **жаловалась**: complained
- **сильнее**: stronger
- **трудностей**: hardships (genitive)
- **хорошо училась**: did well
- **хвалили**: praised
- **участвовала в**: took part in
- **конкурсах**: contests
- **надеялась**: hoped
- **заметит**: will notice
- **а ещё**: and also
- **что**: that
- **поймёт**: will understand
- **кстати**: by the way
- **удивлён**: surprised
- **не думал**: didn't think
- **откажется**: will refuse
- **сильная**: strong
- **был уверен**: was sure
- **бросит**: will give up
- **не произошло**: didn't happen
- **первый курс**: the first year
- **каникулы**: holidays
- **проводить**: spend
- **всё лето**: all summer
- **провели**: spent
- **на даче**: in the country house
- **купались**: bathed
- **загорали**: sunbathed
- **наслаждались**: enjoyed
- **конечно же**: of course
- **на втором курсе**: in the second year
- **нашла**: found
- **детской**: children's
- **зарабатывала больше**: earned more
- **связана**: connected
- **обожали**: adored
- **кажется**: seems
- **чувствовали**: felt
- **на третьем курсе**: in the third year
- **организовать**: organize
- **свою собственную**: her own
- **довольно успешной**: quite successful
- **успех**: success
- **приглашения**: invitations
- **за границей**: abroad
- **доказала**: proved
- **приносит**: brings
- **признал**: admitted
- **улыбка**: smile
- **грустной**: sad

- **eyes**: глаза
- **новые картины**: new paintings
- **однажды**: one day
- **что случилось**: what's happened
- **скучаю**: miss
- **успешная**: successful
- **такая жизнь**: such life
- **не для меня**: not for me
- **в тот вечер**: that evening
- **ещё один**: one more
- **решила**: decided
- **открыть**: open
- **снова**: again
- **учить**: teach
- **стать знаменитой**: become famous
- **делает**: makes
- **других людей**: other people

Questions about the story

1. **Кем хотела стать Аня?**
   What did Ann want to be?

   a. Художницей.
      Painter.

   b. Официанткой.
      Waitress.

   c. Адвокатом.
      Lawyer.

   d. Врачом.
      Doctor.

2. **Кто был против её решения?**
   Who was against her decision?

   a. Друзья.
      Friends.

   b. Отец.
      Father.

   c. Лучшая подруга.
      Best friend.

   d. Учителя.
      Teachers.

3. **Где Аня провела первые каникулы?**
   Where did Ann spend her first holidays?

   a. Дома с родителями.
      At home with her parents.

   b. На выставках.
      At exhibitions.

c. За границей.
   Abroad.

d. На даче с подругой.
   In the country house with her friend.

4. **Друзья организовали для Ани выставку. Правда или ложь?**
   The friends organized an exhibition for Ann. True or false?

   a. Правда.
      True.

   b. Ложь.
      False.

5. **Аня открыла школу для взрослых. Правда или ложь?**
   Ann opened a school for adults. True or false?

   a. Правда.
      True.

   b. Ложь.
      False.

Answers

1. A
2. B
3. D
4. A
5. B

CHAPTER XX

Мой урок. Твой урок —
My Lesson. Your Lesson

Все **родители беспокоятся о** своих **детях**. Они беспокоятся **о здоровье, о развитии**. Кто их **друзья**? **С кем** они **проводят время**? Как они **себя ведут**? Может, их **обижают**? Может, они **одиноки**?

Меня зовут Ирина. Я не **исключение**. Я **уделяю много времени воспитанию** своей **дочери** Саши. Она **активный** и **умный ребёнок**. У меня есть **цель**: Саша **должна** быть **уверена в себе**. Она должна **понимать** — она **личность**.

Но есть **ещё одна вещь**. Ребёнок должен **уважать других людей**: взрослых, друзей. Тебе не нравится **поп-музыка**? **И что**? Она нравится твоему **однокласснику**. У твоей подруги нет **модной одежды**? И что? Её одежда **чистая** и **аккуратная** — этого **достаточно**.

Уважение к себе и уважение к людям — **идеальная комбинация**.

В прошлом году Саша пошла **в первый класс**. Конечно, я волновалась. **Найдёт** ли она друзей? Как она будет **относиться к** одноклассникам? Я **видела**, что она **умеет общаться** с людьми. Она уверена в себе. **А что насчёт других**?

К счастью, я **наткнулась на** интересную **статью** в Интернете. Я **спросила** Сашу:

— **Представь**: ты **обидела человека. Что ты сделаешь?**

— Я **извинюсь**.

— Хорошо, — сказала я. — **Принеси** мне **тюбик зубной пасты** из ванной, пожалуйста.

— **Зачем?**

— **Увидишь.** И ещё **тарелку**.

Саша принесла **вещи**.

— Теперь **выдави** пасту на тарелку.

— **Всю?** — **удивилась** Саша.

— Да, всю.

Скоро вся паста была на тарелке.

— А теперь, — сказала я. — **Затолкай её обратно** в тюбик.

— Как? — Саша **широко раскрыла глаза**.

— Не знаю, **попробуй**.

Саша попробовала, но, конечно, это было **невозможно**.

— Видишь? — спросила я. — Ты можешь обидеть человека. Ты можешь извиниться. Но он будет **чувствовать боль**. Это нельзя **исправить**. **Как** с пастой. Будь **доброй**. **Люби** людей. Это мой **совет**.

Мой **урок произвёл впечатление**. Мы **долго разговаривали**.

Первый год Саши в школе **прошёл хорошо**. Она нашла друзей. Она **хорошо училась**. Я видела, что она добрый ребёнок. Но вчера я **засомневалась**…

Я **зашла** в Сашину **комнату**.

— Смотри, мама, **бабушка** дала мне **два яблока**.

Я **не очень** люблю яблоки. Но я знаю, что очень **важно уметь делиться**.

— **Дай** одно мне, пожалуйста, — попросила я.

Саша взяла **оба**. Она **укусила** одно. **Прожевала, проглотила**. **Затем** она укусила **второе**!

«Моя дочь **жадная**! — подумала я. — Она не хочет делиться. **Даже** со мной! **Что ж**, моя **вина**. Моё воспитание».

Я не знала, что сказать. Саша **подошла ко** мне и сказала:

— **Мамочка**, бери это. Оно **слаще**. Я знаю, ты не любишь **кислые фрукты**.

Я **расплакалась**. Это был урок моей дочери. Для меня. **Не суди** людей. **Не делай выводы** быстро. **Возможно**, ты **просто** не **всё** знаешь.

А яблоко было **действительно вкусным** и сладким...

Краткое содержание истории

У Ирины есть дочь. Её зовут Саша.

Год назад Саша пошла в первый класс. Ирина знала, что Саша уверена в себе. Но как она будет относиться к одноклассникам? Ирина спросила дочку, что Саша сделает, если обидит кого-нибудь. Саша сказала, что она извинится. Ирина попросила Сашу принести тюбик зубной пасты и выдавить его на тарелку. Тогда Ирина попросила Сашу затолкать пасту в тюбик. Это было невозможно. Урок Ирины: можно извиниться, но человек будет чувствовать боль. Важно быть добрым. Важно любить людей.

Вчера Ирина увидела, что у Саши два яблока. Она попросила одно. Саша укусила оба яблока. Ирина подумала, что Саша жадная. Но дочь дала ей одно яблоко и сказала, что оно слаще. Это был урок Саши для Ирины: не суди людей. Возможно, ты просто не всё знаешь.

Summary of the story

Irina has a daughter. Her name is Sasha.

A year ago Sasha went to the first grade. Irina knew that Sasha is self-confident. But how will she treat her classmates? Irina asked her daughter what she would do if she offended someone? Sasha said she'd apologize. Irina asked Sasha to bring her a tube of toothpaste and squeeze the paste onto a plate. Then Irina asked Sasha to push the paste back into the tube. It was impossible. Irina's lesson: one can apologize, but the person will feel pain. It's important to be kind. It's important to love people.

Yesterday Irina saw Sasha had two apples. She asked for one. Sasha bit both the apples. Irina thought Sasha was greedy. But her daughter gave her one apple and said it was sweeter. That was

Sasha's lesson for Irina: don't judge people. Maybe you just don't know everything.

Vocabulary

- **родители**: parents
- **беспокоятся о**: worry about
- **детях**: children (prepositional)
- **о здоровье**: about health
- **о развитии**: about development
- **друзья**: friends
- **с кем**: with whom
- **проводят время**: spend time
- **себя ведут**: behave
- **обижают**: offend
- **одиноки**: lonely (short plural)
- **исключение**: exception
- **уделяю много времени**: devote much time
- **воспитанию**: upbringing (dative)
- **дочери**: daughter (genitive)
- **активный**: active
- **умный**: clever
- **ребёнок**: child
- **цель**: goal
- **должна**: must
- **уверена в себе**: self-confident
- **понимать**: understand
- **личность**: personality
- **ещё одна вещь**: one more thing
- **уважать других людей**: respect other people
- **взрослых**: grownups (genitive)
- **поп-музыка**: pop music
- **и что**: so what
- **однокласснику**: classmate (dative)
- **модной одежды**: fashion clothes (genitive)
- **чистая**: clean
- **аккуратная**: tidy
- **этого достаточно**: that's enough
- **уважение**: respect (noun)
- **идеальная комбинация**: perfect combination
- **в прошлом году**: last year
- **в первый класс**: to first grade
- **найдёт**: will find
- **относится к**: treats
- **видела**: saw

- **умеет общаться**: can communicate
- **а что насчёт других**: and what about others
- **к счастью**: luckily
- **наткнулась на**: came across
- **статью**: article (accusative)
- **спросила**: asked
- **представь**: imagine
- **обидела человека**: offended a person
- **что ты сделаешь**: what will you do
- **извинюсь**: will apologize
- **принеси**: bring (imperative)
- **тюбик зубной пасты**: a toothpaste tube
- **зачем**: what for
- **увидишь**: will see
- **тарелку**: plate
- **вещи**: things
- **выдави**: squeeze
- **всю**: all
- **удивилась**: surprised
- **скоро**: soon
- **затолкай**: push into (imperative)
- **обратно**: back
- **как**: how

- **широко раскрыла глаза**: opened her eyes wide
- **попробуй**: try (imperative)
- **конечно**: of course
- **невозможно**: impossible
- **можешь**: can
- **чувствовать боль**: feel pain
- **исправить**: fix
- **как**: like
- **доброй**: kind
- **люби**: love (imperative)
- **совет**: advice
- **урок**: lesson
- **произвёл впечатление**: made an impression
- **долго разговаривали**: were talking for a long time
- **первый год**: first year
- **прошёл хорошо**: went well
- **хорошо училась**: did well
- **засомневалась**: started having doubts
- **зашла**: entered
- **комнату**: room (accusative)
- **бабушка**: grandmother
- **два яблока**: two apples
- **не очень**: not much

- **важно**: important
- **уметь**: be able to
- **делиться**: share
- **дай**: give (imperative)
- **оба**: both
- **укусила**: bit
- **прожевала**: chewed
- **проглотила**: swallowed
- **затем**: then
- **второе**: the other
- **жадная**: greedy
- **даже**: even
- **что ж**: well
- **вина**: fault
- **подошла ко**: went up to
- **мамочка**: mummy
- **это**: this one
- **слаще**: sweeter
- **кислые фрукты**: sour fruit
- **расплакалась**: burst out crying
- **не суди**: don't judge (imperative)
- **не делай выводы**: don't make conclusions (imperative)
- **возможно**: maybe
- **просто**: just
- **всё**: everything
- **действительно**: really
- **вкусным**: tasty

Questions about the story

1. **Ирина считает, что Саша должна...**
   Irina thinks that Sasha must...

   a. Уважать себя и других людей.
      Respect herself and other people.

   b. Уважать только себя.
      Respect herself only.

   c. Бояться других людей.
      Be afraid of other people.

   d. Уметь извиняться.
      Be able to apologize.

2. **Где Ирина прочитала про урок с зубной пастой?**
   Where has Irina read about the lesson with the toothpaste?

   a. В книге.
   b. In a book.

   c. В журнале.
   d. In a magazine.

   e. В газете.
   f. In a newspaper.

   g. В Интернете.
   h. On the Net.

3. **Мамин урок не произвёл на Сашу впечатления. Правда или ложь?**
   Mother's lesson didn't make an impression on Sasha. True or false?

   a. Правда.
      True.

b. Ложь.

False.

4. **Ирина попросила Сашу дать ей одно яблоко, потому что...**

Irina asked Sasha to give her one apple because...

a. Она очень любит яблоки.

She loves apples a lot.

b. Саше нельзя есть много яблок.

Sasha isn't allowed to eat many apples.

c. Она хотела научить дочку делиться.

She wanted to teach her daughter to share.

d. Она знала, что яблоко сладкое.

She knew the apple was sweet.

5. **Саша была жадной. Правда или ложь?**

Sasha was greedy. True or false?

a. Правда.

True.

b. Ложь.

False.

Answers

1. A
2. D
3. B
4. C
5. B

MORE FROM LINGO MASTERY

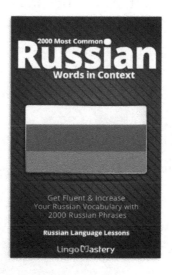

Have you been trying to learn Russian and simply can't find the way to expand your vocabulary?

Do your teachers recommend you boring textbooks and complicated stories that you don't really understand?

Are you looking for a way to learn the language quicker without taking shortcuts?

If you answered *"Yes!"* to at least one of those previous questions, then this book is for you! We've compiled the **2000 Most Common Words in Russian,** a list of terms that will expand your vocabulary to levels previously unseen.

Did you know that — according to an important study — learning the top two thousand (2000) most frequently used words will enable you to understand up to **84%** of all non-fiction and **86.1%** of fiction literature and **92.7%** of oral speech? Those are *amazing* stats, and this book will take you even further than those numbers!

In this book:

- A detailed introduction with tips and tricks on how to improve your learning
- A list of **2000** of the most common words in Russian and their translations
- An example sentence for each word – in both Russian *and* English
- Finally, a conclusion to make sure you've learned and supply you with a final list of tips

Don't look any further, we've got what you need right here!

In fact, we're ready to turn you into a Russian speaker... are you ready to become one?

CONCLUSION

We hope you've enjoyed our stories and the way we've presented them. Each chapter, as you will have noticed, was a way to practice a language tool that you will regularly use when speaking Russian.

Never forget: learning a language doesn't *have* to be a boring activity if you find the proper way to do it. Hopefully, we've provided you with a hands-on, fun way to expand your knowledge in Russian, and you can apply your lessons to future ventures.

Feel free to use this book further ahead when you need to go back to remembering vocabulary and expressions — in fact, we encourage it.

Believe in yourself and never be ashamed to make mistakes. Even the best can fall; it's those who get up that can achieve greatness! Take care!

PS: Keep an eye out for more books like this one; we're not done teaching you Russian! Head over to www.LingoMastery.com and read our articles and sign up for our newsletter. We give away so much free stuff that will accelerate your Russian learning, and you don't want to miss that!

CPSIA information can be obtained
at www.ICGtesting.com
Printed in the USA
LVHW020404160820
663214LV00001B/1

9 781951 949006